FINANCIAL ACCOUNTING AND REPORTING STUDY GUIDE NOTES

LEONARD PRATHER

authorHOUSE®

AuthorHouse™
1663 Liberty Drive
Bloomington, IN 47403
www.authorhouse.com
Phone: 1 (800) 839-8640

Published by AuthorHouse 09/12/2017

ISBN: 978-1-5462-0528-9 (sc)
ISBN: 978-1-5462-0527-2 (e)

Library of Congress Control Number: 2017912916

Print information available on the last page.

Any people depicted in stock imagery provided by Thinkstock are models, and such images are being used for illustrative purposes only. Certain stock imagery © Thinkstock.

This book is printed on acid-free paper.

CONTENTS

ABBREVIATIONS AND ACRONYMS

Here are some common abbreviations used throughout the text.

AJE - adjusting journal entry
AP - accounts payable
AR - accounts receivable
BD - bad debt
BS - balance sheet
CF - cash flow
DL - direct labor
Exp - expense
FA - fixed assets
FS - financial statement
FV - fair value
GAAP - generally accepted accounting principles
GAAPro - generally accepted auditing procedures
GAAS - generally accepted auditing standards
IRS - internal revenue service
IS - income statement
JE - journal entry
NBV - net book value
NI - net income
NP - notes payable
OH - overhead
o/s - outstanding
PV - present value
RE - retained earnings
RM - raw material
SFAC - statement of financial accounting concepts
SFAS - statement of financial accounting standards
SOP - statement of position
TB - trial balance
w/o - write off
WP - work papers
WS - work sheet

AICPA - American Institute of Certified Public Accountants
ASC - Accounting Standards Codification
APB - Accounting Principle Board
APBO - Accounting Principle Board Opinion
ARB - Accounting Research Bulletin
EITF - Emerging Issues Task Force
FASB - Financial Accounting Standards Board

ACCOUNTING BASICS

Subsequent Event
- *After* balance-sheet date and
- *Before* financial statements are issued.

Record Short-Term Debt as Long-Term Debt
- When a financial agreement has been accepted;
- For the purpose of refinancing;
- Short-term debt on a long-term basis—for example, debt or equity securities issued on a long-term basis.

Accounting Equation

Assets = Liabilities + Capital

Current assets
- Current liabilities
Working capital

Accounting Cycle

Daily transactions are posted to *journals* (double entry); debits and credits are recorded.

↓

Adjusting entries are entered and posted.

↓

Closing entries (closing of nominal accounts) are entered and posted. This is a year-end or period function.

↓

Trial balance is generated.

↓

Financial statements (income statement, balance sheet, cash flow, change in stockholders' equity) are prepared.

↓

Cycle repeats.

Cash to Accrual Basis

Accrual Basis	Deferral Basis
Revenue recognized when earned.	Unearned revenue collected in advance.
Expense recognized when incurred.	Expense prepaid in advance.

Transaction	Activity	Accrual Basis	Cash Basis
Revenue	Payment	Decrease—receivable	Revenue recognized
Expense	Payment	Decrease—payable	Expense incurred
Prepaid Revenue	Payment	Record—liability	Revenue recognized
Prepaid Expense	Payment	Record—asset	Expense incurred

Cash basis (not GAAP)

Record revenue or expense when cash is collected or paid.

There is no receivable or payable.

There is no inventory.

There is improper matching of revenue and expense.

Accrual basis (GAAP accounting)

Record revenue or expense when earned or incurred.

Receivable and payable exist.

Inventory is maintained.

There is proper matching of revenue and expense.

Prepaid

Prepaid *revenue* is a liability, properly stated.

Prepaid *expense* is an asset, properly stated.

Prepaid revenue

Overstates income.

Overstates net income

Understates liabilities.

Prepaid Expense

Overstates expense.

Understates net income.

Understates assets.

Nominal (temporary) **accounts** relate to income statement accounts and are closed at year end to income summary.

Real (permanent) **accounts** relate to balance-sheet accounts and are *not* closed at year end. These balances are cumulative.

Posting Journals
- Sales journal (records sales activity)
- Cash receipt journal (records cash transactions)
- Accounts payable journal (records vendor activity)
- Purchase journal (records purchases)
- General journal includes transactions not related to any of the above journals.

Closing entries are posted at year end to close nominal accounts.

Sales accounts $$.$$

     Income summary $$.$$

Income summary $$.$$

     Expense accounts $$.$$

Retained earnings $$.$$

    Income summary $$.$$

Adjusting entries are posted regularly throughout the accounting cycle.
- Accruals
- Prepaid
- Estimates
- Reversing entries, which reverse in a subsequent period.

Accruals are earned or incurred transactions.
- Accrued revenue—example: rent revenue
- Accrued asset— example: rent receivable
- Accrued expense—example: salaries expense
- Accrued liability— example: salaries payable

Prepaid
- **Prepaid expense** is an expense paid in advance (e.g., insurance)
  - o   It is classified as an asset on the balance sheet. (It is represented as a current and/or noncurrent asset on the balance sheet.)
  - o   The expense is recorded when incurred.
- **Prepaid revenue** is income paid in advance (e.g., rental income)
  - o   It is classified as a liability on the balance sheet. (It is represented as a current and/or noncurrent liability on the balance sheet.)
  - o   The revenue is recorded when earned.

Understanding Account Interaction

This is useful when solving for an unknown value.

Retained earnings (RE)—Beginning   **Dividend payable**—Beginning

Net income (NI)   Dividend declared

- Dividend declared   —Dividend paid

Ending retained earnings   Ending dividend payable

Income tax payable—Beginning   **Deferred tax**—Beginning

Provision   Provision

- Payment   - Payment

Ending income tax payable   Ending deferred tax

Inventory—Beginning   **Accounts payable (AP)**—Beginning

Purchases   Purchases

- Cost of sales   - Payments

Ending inventory   Ending accounts payable

Accounts receivable (AR)—Beg   **Income statement**

Sale   Sales

- Payments   - Cost of sales

+ Write-off/adjustments   Gross profit

Ending accounts receivable

Bond Payable—Beginning

Bond issue

- Bond redemption

Bond payable - Ending

Determine the Cost or Proceeds of an Asset Sale

       Proceeds

       – Net book value

       Gain/loss on disposal

1. Proceeds = Net book value + Gain
2. Proceeds = Net book value – Loss
3. Cost = Proceeds – Gain
4. Cost = Proceeds + Loss

ACCOUNTING FOR CHANGING PRICES

Monetary
- Assets and liabilities are fixed dollar amounts.
- They do not change with changes in dollar value (purchasing power).
- Unrealized gains/losses are holding purchasing-power gains and losses.
- Items include
  - Receivables
  - Payables
  - Cash and cash equivalents
  - Nonconvertible preferred stock

Example:
A holder of a $10,000 promissory note entered into ten years ago and due today will receive $10,000 even though the value of $10,000 today is less than its value ten years ago. This change in dollar value is referred to as unrealized purchasing-power gain or loss.

Nonmonetary
- Assets and liabilities dollar amounts are *not* fixed.
  - They fluctuate with changes in specific price levels.
  - They fluctuate with changes in general purchasing power (CPI).
- Price changes are due to
  - Fair market value (FMV)—specific price-level changes
    - Appreciation
    - Depreciation
  - Consumer Price Index (CPI)—general price-level changes
    - Inflation
    - Deflation
- Examples:
  - Inventory
  - Property, plant, and equipment
  - Land
  - Common stock
  - Deferred assets and liabilities
  - Investment in subsidiary
  - Advance receipts

Example:
A purchaser of 10,000 shares of Company XYZ ten years ago.

Ten years ago, he was subject to
- *Changes in purchasing power (Consumer Price Index—CPI)*
- *Rise or fall in fair market value*

Today, if the change in purchasing power (Consumer Price Index—CPI) was offset by equivalent change in fair market value, then the price of the shares is the same as it was ten year ago.

	Inflation	Deflation
Asset	Loss	Gain
Liability	Gain	Loss

During Inflation	Monetary	Nonmonetary
Asset	Loss	Gain
Liability	Gain	Loss

Monetary (Fixed dollar amount)

Cash and cash equivalents

Receivables

Payables

Investments—debt and equity securities

Nonmonetary (Dollar fluctuates)

Property, plant and equipment

Accumulation/amortization

Inventory

Building

Land

Stockholders' equity

Intangibles

Revenue and expense items

Monetary - During inflation, price index increases and dollar value decreases.
For example, $1 is now worth 90 cents
- Asset: If you are owed $1 when the value of the dollar is worth 90 cents, you will have a 10-cent loss**.**
- Liability: If you have to pay $1 when the value of the dollar is 90 cents, you will have a 10-cent gain.

Nonmonetary - During Inflation, price index increases and dollar value decreases.
For example,. $1 is now worth .90 cents
- o Asset: A product sold for a $1.00 now sells for $1.10. The same product, if resold, will yield you a 10-cent gain.
- o Liability: If you owed $1, you will now pay $1.10. The payment will yield you a 10-cent loss.

Financial Reporting and Changing Prices
ASC 255 (SFAS 89)
Applies to foreign entities in countries with hyperinflationary economies that prepare financial statements for businesses preparing US GAAP (generally accepted accounting practices) financial statements.
> Note: Hyperinflationary economy is the consumption of goods and services in a geographical location with accelerating rates of inflation that cause the currency to lose value.

Codification is not required, but voluntary disclosure is encouraged as supplemental information.
The effects of changing prices relating to GAAP prepared financial statements require the use of CPI-U (Consumer Price Index of Urban Consumer).

Inflation results in a loss of currency purchasing power or value.

Purchasing power is the purchasing value of a dollar—in other words, the worth of a dollar.

Purchasing power gain or loss is the effect of changes in dollar value on monetary assets and liabilities.

Price Level Changes

Fluctuations effect

- General Price Changes: The Consumer Price Index (CPI) is the overall measure of goods and services representing economic changes in consumer prices.
- Specific Price Changes
  - Internal influences
  - External influences: Third-party price increases affect your business.
  - Direct Pricing of Goods/Services
    - Current cost
    - Vendor prices
    - Manufacturing cost

Consumer Price Index (CPI) for **Urban Consumer** (CPI-U)

- Urban price index is used.
- Purchasing power is the value of a dollar adjusted for inflation.

Inflation is the increase in cost of consumer products; as the cost of products increase, the purchasing value of a dollar decreases.

The consumer price index

- Is an economic factor;
- Measures overall goods and services;
- Reflects the purchasing power of a dollar.

$$\frac{\text{Current year—CPI-U}}{\text{Base year CPI-U}} = \text{Consumer Price Index (CPI-U)}$$

Types of Pricing

- Historical cost is the actual cost.
- Current cost is fair value (FV).
- Consumer price index (CPI) is actual (historical) cost adjusted for CPI.
- Nominal is historical cost that has not been adjusted for FV or CPI.

Historical Cost (Nominal Dollar)

- Actual purchase cost
- Original purchase or sale price
- No adjustment for general or specific prices changes

Nominal Dollar

- Historical cost
- Actual purchase price
- Not adjusted for changes in dollar value (no fair-value or CPI adjustments)

Current Cost

- Current purchase price;
- Includes specific price changes, stated at the lower of one of the following:
  - Current cost (fair value)
  - Replacement (recoverable) cost.
- Gains and losses (G/L) are recognized.

Current cost
– <u>Historical cost</u>
Unrealized holding gain or loss (G/L) recognized.

Constant Dollar
- Includes general price changes.
- Historic (nominal) or current cost is adjusted for inflation.
    - Monetary assets and liabilities (A&L) are not restated for general price changes (changes in dollar value). Purchasing power—unrealized G/L are recognized.
        - Examples:
            - Cash
            - Accounts receivable
            - Notes receivable
            - Accounts payable
            - Notes payable
            - Bonds payable
    - Nonmonetary asset and liabilities (A&L)
        - Restate for general price changes (changes in dollar value).
        - Purchasing Power—unrealized G/L are *not* recognized.
            - examples:
                - Inventory
                - Property
                - Plant and equipment
                - Deferred revenue

        Constant dollar
        – <u>Historical cost</u>
        Inflation factor

Pricing Measurements
1. Historical cost/nominal dollar
2. Historical cost/constant dollar
3. Current cost/nominal dollar
4. Current cost/constant dollar

Historical Cost/Nominal Dollar
- Includes no specific or general price changes;
- Is *not* adjusted to
    - Current cost or
    - Constant dollar.
No purchasing-power gains or losses are recognized.

Example:
Historic building that cost $10,000 is reported as $10,000.

Historical Cost/Constant Dollar
- *Includes general price level changes.*
- *Adjusted for general price-level changes.*
- *Monetary assets and liabilities are not restated.*
- *Unrealized gains and losses recognized.*

- *Nonmonetary* assets and liabilities are restated.
- Unrealized gains and losses **not** recognized.

Disclosure example:
- Historic: building that cost $10,000 is reported as $10,000.
- Constant dollar: building cost is $11,000 (10,000 * 1.10 CPI)
- Gains/losses recognized: none
- Inflationary factor: $1,000

$$
\begin{aligned}
&\text{Constant dollar } \$\,11,000 \\
&\underline{-\ \text{Historical cost } 10,000} \\
&\textbf{Inflation factor } \$\,\textbf{1,000}
\end{aligned}
$$

Current Cost/Nominal Dollar
- Includes specific price level changes.
- Historic cost stated at whichever is lower:
    - Current (fair value)
    - Replacement cost
- General price changes are not applicable.
- Current cost is *not* adjusted for general price level changes.

Example:
- Historic Cost: building that cost $10,000 is reported as $10,000.
- Specific dollar: building cost is $15,000 (FV) on balance sheet disclosure.
- Factors increase the cost to $15,000.
- G/L recognized: $5,000 on income statement disclosure as part of income from continuing operations.
- Inflationary factor: none

Current Cost/Constant Dollar
- Includes specific and general price level changes.
- Historic cost is adjusted for:
    - Current (fair values)
    - CPI

Disclosure example
- Historic cost: building cost $10,000 is reported as $10,000.
- Specific cost (current cost): building. cost: $15,000 (FV)   balance sheet disclosure.
    - Gains/ losses recognized: $4,000   income statement disclosure.
        - Current cost **minus** constant dollar cost = Gains/losses recognized.
        - As part of Income from continuing operations.
- General cost (constant dollar): building cost: $11,000 (CPI) balance sheet disclosure.
    - $11,000 = 10,000 * 1.10 CPI
    - Inflationary factor: $1,000

Overview

	Inflation (CPI)	**Appreciation** (FMV)	**Comment**
Historical cost/ nominal $	No	No	Historic value *not* adjusted for Consumer Price Index and fair market value.
Historical cost/ constant $	Yes	No	Historic value adjusted for Consumer Price Index and fair market value.
Current cost/ constant $	No	Yes	Current value not adjusted for Consumer Price Index and fair market value.
Current cost/ constant $	Yes	Yes	Current value adjusted for Consumer Price Index and fair market value.

Reporting example—Current Cost

Income Statement

3,000 sales units x current - unit cost $65 = sales at current cost $195,000

3,000 sales units x average— current - unit cost $115 = sales at current cost $345,000

Cost of goods sold $2,000 x average—current - unit cost $115 = Cost of goods sold at current cost $230,000

$$Average— current - unit cost \ \$115 = \frac{(beginning\ \$110 + ending\ \$120)}{2\ periods— beginning\ and\ ending}$$

Balance Sheet
- *Appreciable assets are stated at current cost.*
- *Depreciable assets are an average of current cost and purchase price:*

$$\frac{Purchase\ price\ \$335 + Current\ cost\ \$355}{2\ periods—beginning\ and\ ending} = Depreciable\ basis\ \$345,000$$

$$\frac{Depreciable\ basis\ (\$345,000)}{Useful\ life\ (5\ years)} = Depreciation\ expense\ \$69,000$$

- *Inventory:*

Ending QOH 70 x current - unit cost $61 = E—inventory $4,270

Reporting example—Constant Dollar

Income Statement

$$\text{Sales Units } 3{,}000 \times \frac{\underline{\text{CPI—current } \$130}}{\text{CPI—average } \$120} = \text{Sales at constant } \$\ \$3{,}250$$

$$\text{CPI—average } \$120 = \frac{\underline{\text{CPI—beginning } \$110 + \text{CPI—ending } \$130}}{2 \text{ periods— beginning and ending}}$$

Balance Sheet

Appreciable assets: calculating purchase price ($520)

$$\text{Purchase price } \$400 \times \frac{\underline{\text{CPI—Current year } \$130}}{\text{CPI – Prior year } \$100} = \text{Assets at constant dollar } \$520$$

Depreciable assets: cost $400
                           —Accumulated 240
                      Net book value $160

Net book value $160 × $\dfrac{\underline{\text{CPI—current } \$130}}{\text{CPI - at purchase date } \$110}$ = Net book value at constant dollar $189

If sold.

	Proceeds	$200
Less	NBV at constant	- $189
	Gain/loss recognized	$ 11

Example:

Jan 2017 Land:	$10,000 purchase price
Fair value	$18,000
CPI	10% Price increase 10% during year.

	Balance Sheet	**Income Statement**
Historical Cost/Nominal $		
Land:	$10,000	0

Depreciation: straight line 5 years

$$\text{Constant } \$: \frac{\underline{\$10{,}000}}{5 \text{ years}} = \$2{,}000 \text{ Historical depreciation expense}$$

$$\underline{\text{Depreciation:}} \quad \frac{\underline{\text{Historical } \$}}{\text{Useful Life}} = \text{Historical depreciation expense}$$

Historic Cost/Constant $

Land: $11,000   0

Historic adjusted for change in $ value: $10,000 x 1.10
Historic times CPI ratio

Depreciation: SL 5 years

$$\text{Constant \$: } \frac{\$11,000}{5 \text{ years}} = \$2,200 \text{ Constant \$ depreciation expense}$$

$$\text{Depreciation: } \frac{\text{Constant \$}}{\text{Useful Life}} = \text{Constant \$ depreciation expense}$$

Current Cost/Nominal $

	Balance Sheet	Income Statement
Land:	$18,000	$8,000 Unrealized gain recognized
	Current cost	Current minus Historic = Unrealized gain recognized
		$18,000 minus 10,000 = $8,000 Unrealized gain recognized

Depreciation: straight line 5 years

$$\text{Constant \$: } \frac{\$18,000}{5 \text{ years}} = \$3,600 \text{ current cost depreciation expense}$$

Current cost depreciation expense times average purchase periods = constant $ depreciation expense

$$\text{Depreciation: } \frac{\text{constant \$}}{\text{Useful life}} = \text{Constant \$ depreciation expense}$$

Current Cost/Constant $

Land:	$18,000	$7,000 unrealized gain recognized
	Current cost	current minus constant = unrealized gain recognized
		$18,000 minus 11,000 = $7,000 unrealized gain recognized

ACCOUNTING FOR INCOME TAXES

Overview

Net Income per Book
+ or - permanent differences
<u>+ or - temporary difference</u> x future tax rate = deferred tax asset or liability
taxable income (TI) x current tax rate = Income Tax Payable
<u>+</u>   Alternative Minimum Tax or credit
+   Personal holding tax
+   Environment tax
Less: foreign tax credit or business credits
<u>Less: payments</u>
            Tax liability or refund

Income Tax Payable

Income tax expense	$$$	
Income tax payable		$$$

Deferred Tax Asset (DTA)

DTA—Current	$$$	
DTA—Noncurrent	$$$	
Deferred tax expense		$$$
(or Income tax expense)		

Deferred Tax Liability (DTL)

Deferred tax expense	$$$	
(or income tax expense)		
DTL—Current		$$$
DTL—Noncurrent		$$$

Accounting for income tax is a method of calculating and accounting for income tax payable, deferred taxes, and related expenses as outlined in Accounting Standard Code (ASC) 740.
1. Permanent differences
    a. Have no deferred tax effect
    b. Are added or subtracted from net income to arrive at taxable income
    c. Affect book or tax calculation only, not both

2. Temporary differences
    a. Affect *both* book and tax calculations
    b. produce a deferred tax Asset (DTA) or deferred tax liability (DTL) based on

      i.   The item being adjusted.

      ii.   Its balance sheet classification.

  c.   The DTA or DTL is computed using the *future tax rate* times the adjusted amount

3. Income tax reporting
   a. Under GAAP, deferred tax is reported as current or noncurrent.
   b. Deferred tax asset and liability are netted.
      i. Current DTA and DTL are netted.
      ii. Noncurrent DTA and DTL are netted.

Current	Noncurrent (LT)
DTA	DTA
- DTL	- DTL
Net	**Net**

Permanent Differences

Description	Difference	Classification
Goodwill is not amortized for book (tested for impairment)	Permanent	
Goodwill is amortized (15 years) for tax vs. book amortization	Permanent	
Charitable contribution vs. allowed charitable deduction = nondeductible	Permanent	
Interest income—muni bonds—nontaxable	Permanent	
Interest expense—muni bonds—nondeductible	Permanent	
DRD—dividend received deduction—tax deduction, not book deduction.	Permanent	
Life insurance premium expense—officers—nondeductible	Permanent	
Life insurance proceeds—officers—nontaxable	Permanent	
Federal income tax provision—nondeductible	Permanent	
Meals and entertainment expenses— 50% nondeductible	Permanent	
Capital loss vs. capital gains is nondeductible	Permanent	
Penalties and fines are not deductible for tax	Permanent	
Temporary Differences		

Description	Difference	Classification
Organization cost - amortized (15 years) tax vs. book (expensed)	Temporary	DTA
Depreciation expense (tax) vs. book	Temporary	DTL
Bad debt provision (book)—nondeductible for tax	Temporary	DTA
Actual bad debt write-off (tax)—deductible for tax	Temporary	DTL
Gain on involuntary conversion	Temporary	DTL
Accrued losses vs. deductible amount	Temporary	DTA
Prepaid expense (tax) vs. accrual (book)	Temporary	DTL
Warranty accrual (book) vs. actual warranty expense (tax)	Temporary	DTA
Prepaid revenue (tax) vs. accrued (book)	Temporary	DTA
Accrual sale (book) vs. installment sale (tax)	Temporary	DTL
% Complete (book) vs. completed contract (tax)	Temporary	DTL
NOL at 100% - balance carry forward	Temporary	DTA

Examples of transactions that are recognized before or after book.

Prepaid revenue is recognized before book.
Prepaid expense is recognized before book.
Long-term contracts are completed as opposed to % complete. Completed contract revenue is recognized after book.
Warranty cost is the actual warranty cost deducted for income tax calculation. Warranty expense accrual is not deductible for tax.

Summary

Accrual Tax	vs.	Book		Taxable Income	Reporting period - Current	Reporting period - Future
Expense—tax	>	Book expense	=	Subtract	DTL	DTA
Expense—tax	<	Book expense	=	Add	DTA	DTL
Revenue—tax	>	Book revenue	=	Add	DTA	DTL
Revenue—tax	<	Book revenue	=	Subtract	DTL	DTA

Deferrals Tax	vs.	Book		Taxable Income	Reporting Period—Current	Reporting Period—Future
Prepaid expense— tax (cash paid)	>	Book expense (Accrual)	=	Subtract	DTL	DTA
Prepaid expense— tax (cash paid)	<	Book expense (Accrual)	=	Add	DTA	DTL
Prepaid revenue—tax (cash collected)	>	Book revenue (Accrual)	=	Add	DTA	DTL
Prepaid revenue—tax (cash collected)	<	Book revenue (Accrual)	=	Subtract	DTL	DTA

Example:

Net Income per book $100.00
<u>+ *Permanent differences -20.00*</u>
<u>+ *Temporary differences -35.00*</u>
TI *(Taxable Income) 45.00*
   <u>– *State income tax expense - 8.00*</u>
   TI after state tax deduction *37.00*
   x <u>*FIT (federal income tax) rate x 32%*</u>
   Federal tax liability/expense 11.84
   <u>– *Estimated FIT Payment—**9.50***</u>
   Current federal tax liability *$ 2.34*

Journal entry to record:

Income tax expense
*Income Tax Expense $**11.84***
          Income Tax Payable   *11.84*

Estimated tax payment
*Income Tax Payable $**9.50***
       Cash   *9.50*

Temporary difference x Future tax rate = Deferred tax liability

   -$35   *x*   *30%* ⁼ *$10.50*

Book depreciation exceeded tax depreciation by $35. Therefore, the excess depreciation creates income that leads to a deferred tax liability in the current period.

Deferred Tax Asset
  Deferred tax asset $.$$
       Income tax expense—deferred $.$$

Deferred Tax Liability
Income tax expense—deferred $10.50
       Deferred tax liability   10.50

Investment in Investee or Subsidiary

Deferred Tax Calculation—Undistributed Income or Earnings

  Income from investment $210 x 30% = $ 63
  <u>– Dividend received   60 x 30% = - 18</u>
  Undistributed earnings   150 $45 x 80% DRD = $14.40 Nontaxable dividend
  <u>– Dividend received deduction   - 36</u>
  Undistributed Earnings $ 9 x 35% (Deferred tax rate) = $3.15 DTL

Income Tax Calculation—Income from Investment

Income from investment $210 x 30% = $ 63
<u>– Dividend received—60</u> x 30% = <u>- 18</u> x 80% DRD = $14.40 Nontaxable Div.
Undistributed earnings 150

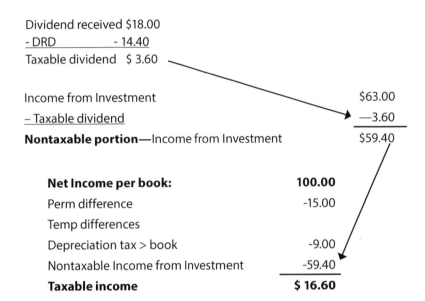

Dividend received $18.00
<u>- DRD   - 14.40</u>
Taxable dividend $ 3.60

Income from Investment	$63.00
<u>– Taxable dividend</u>	<u>—3.60</u>
Nontaxable portion—Income from Investment	$59.40

Net Income per book:	**100.00**
Perm difference	-15.00
Temp differences	
Depreciation tax > book	-9.00
Nontaxable Income from Investment	<u>-59.40</u>
Taxable income	**$ 16.60**

Net Operating Loss (NOL)

1. Net operating loss is negative net income.
    a. Carryback (2 years)—produces an Income tax receivable (reduces prior year income).
    b. Carryforward (20 years)— produces a deferred tax asset (reduces future income).

Example—NOL Effect

<u>Tax rate</u>
Back (2 years)—$40 x 30% = Income tax receivable $12.00
NOL   - $115
          Forward (20 years) - $75 x 35% = Deferred tax asset $26.25

Recording Tax Effect of NOL Carryback and Forward
 Income tax receivable $12.00

  DTA   26.25
     Income tax expense—Deferred 38.25

Recording Tax Effect of NOL Carry Forward (only)
  DTA   26.25
     Income tax expense—deferred 26.25

Valuation Allowance
1. Is recorded when a portion or all of the Deferred Tax Asset (DTA) will not be realized.

Calculate Valuation Allowance

Valuation Allowance = Deferred tax asset x Allowance provision

$9	=	$30	x	3%	

Record Valuation Allowance

Income tax expense—Valuation allowance $9
    Valuation allowance—Deferred tax asset $9

BONDS

1. Bond
   a. Issuer (Seller)
      i. Sells a bond.
         1. Records a bond payable
            a. Using gross method
               i. No gain or loss (G/L) recognized
            b. Or fair value method
               i. G/L is recognized
   b. Bond issue cost
      i. Is the cost of selling the bond recorded by seller.
         1. Is amortized over life of bond.
   c. Purchaser (buyer or bondholder)
      i. Records investment in bond using either/or:
         1. Gross method - discount or premium account is used
            a. Discount
               i. Stated rate (bond rate) < Yield (market rate)
               ii. Investor receives less interest than what the market is offering.
               iii. May not be an attractive offer
            b. Premium
               i. Stated rate (bond rate) > Yield (market rate)
               ii. Investor receives more interest than what the market is offering
               iii. May be an attractive offer
            c. Face Value
               i. Stated rate (bond rate) = Yield (market rate)
               ii. Investor receives interest equal to the market rate
               iii. A good offer
         2. Net method - No discount or premium account is used.
2. Bond amortization method
   a. Straight line (SL) method (non-GAAP)
      i. Amortization expense is the same over the life of the bond at a premium or discount.
      ii. Unamortized bond discount balance is understated; balance decreases over time.
      iii. Unamortized bond premium balance is understated; balance decreases over time.
      iv. Book value of bond recorded at a discount is overstated; book value increases over time to reach face amount.
      v. Book value of bond recorded at a premium is understated; book value decreases over time to reach face amount
   b. Effective interest method (GAAP)
      i. Amortization expense increases over the life of the bond at a premium or discount.
      ii. Unamortized bond balance at a discount is properly stated; balance decreases over time to reach face amount.
      iii. Unamortized bond balance at a premium is properly stated; balance decreases over time to reach face amount.
      iv. Book value of bond at a discount is properly stated; book value increases over time to reach face amount.

        v.   Book value of bond at a premium is properly stated; book value decreases over time to reach face amount

3. Bond accounting
    a. Trading
        i. Bond is neither held to maturity nor available for sale.
        ii. Gains and losses are recognized as part of income from continuing operations.
    b. Held to maturity (HTM)—discount or premium account is used to record bond for seller or buyer.
        1. The bond is amortized over life of bond using the effective interest method.
        2. No gain or loss is recognized unless the fair value method is used.
    c. Fair value
        i. Bond is recorded at fair market value.
        ii. No discount or premium account is used to record bond.
        1. Amortized bond over life of bond using effective interest method is optional.
        2. Gains or Losses are recognized as part of income from continuing operations.
4. Bond sinking fund
    a. An account is set up to pay off the bond at maturity.
    b. Financial statement (FS) reporting
        i. Balance sheet—reports the sinking fund in the long term or other assets category.
        ii. Income statement—reports the amortized discount, premium or realized gain or loss.
        iii. Footnote disclosure— the schedule shows a 5-year forecast, indicating:
            1. Maturity dates
            2. Bond requirements
            3. Amount due at maturity
5. Types of bonds
    a. Held to maturity— the bond is held to maturity and amortized over the life of the bond.
    b. Term bond—the bond matures on a specific date.
    c. Serial bond—the bond has multiple maturities.
    d. Callable bond (redeemed)—bond issuer may redeem and/or retire the bond.
    e. Convertible bond—the bond holder (purchaser) has right to convert the bond to stock.
    f. Debenture—this is an unsecured bond.
    g. Bond with detachable stock warrants—the bond issued with stock warrants.
6. Bond issue cost
    a. A deferred charge
    b. Categorized as "other assets" in the balance sheet
    c. Amortized using straight line (SL) method over the life of the bond from date of issue to maturity

Example:

ABC Company incurred bond issue cost of $11,700 for a 10 yr. bond dated January 1, 2017 and issued April 1, 2017.

Printing	*$1,000*
Engraving	*500*
Legal and accounting	*7,000*
Commissions	*2,000*
Underwriter	*1,200*
Total:	***$11,700***

Example:

Issue cost $11,700

Date of bond: 1/1 3 months is not included in the amortization calculation
Issue date: 4/1

Life of bond: 10 yrs x 12 months = 120
<u>*From date of bond to issue date   -3*</u>
Amortization period - Months   117

Recording Bond Issue Cost

Bond Issue Cost	$11,700
Cash / Accts Payable	11,600

Each bond issue cost is recorded when occurred.

Calculating Amortization of Bond Issue Cost

Bond issue cost	$11,700	= Bond issue expense $100 per month
Life of bond from bond issue date	117	

Record Bond Issue Cost Amortized Expense

Bond issue expense	$100
Bond issue cost	$100

Umamortized Bond Issue Cost Balance

Bond issue Cost	$11,700
- Bond issue expense	- 100
Unamortized bond issue Cost	$11,600

Bond Issue Price

Determine bond issue price using one of the following methods:
1. Present value (PV) method
    a. At par—bond rate (coupon or stated rate) = market rate (yield rate)
    b. At discount—bond rate (coupon or stated rate) < market rate (yield rate)
    c. At premium—bond rate (coupon or stated rate) > market rate (yield rate)   seller (issuer)
2. Percentage or rate factor method or
    a. At par—bond rate (coupon or stated rate) = market rate (yield rate)
    b. At discount—bond rate (coupon or stated rate) < market rate (yield rate)   purchaser (bondholder)
    c. At premium—bond rate (coupon or stated rate) > market rate (yield rate)

Bond Held to Maturity (HTM)
    a. Record using present value (PV) method or percentage factor method
    b. A bond discount or premium is recorded.
    c. Amortize the bond discount or premium using the effective interest method.
    d. No gain or loss (G/L) is recognized.

e. If, the fair value (FV) method is elected, record the bod at FV.
    i. Book value (BV) of the bond is adjusted to fair value.
    ii. FV method is not required. But, maybe elected.
    iii. The election is made at origination date.
    iv. Once elected cannot be changed.
    v. No bond discount or premium is recorded.
    vi. Unrealized gain or loss is recognized in the income statement (difference between FV and BV).
    vii. Amortize BV of bond using effective interest method or a different method if preferred.

Two Methods for calculating Bond Issue Selling Price

1. **Present Value (PV) Method**

Bond principle amount   =   bond face amount   x   PV of 1 at market rate

+ Accrued interest   =   bond face amount   x   bond–interest rate   x   PV of annuity due or ordinary

Bond issue price   Annuity at market rate

Determining PV Factor			
Description	**Annual**	**Semiannual**	**Quarterly**
Bond (coupon) **rate**	x 1	divide by 2	divide by 4
Yield (market) **rate**	x 1	divide by 2	divide by 4
Bond Life	x 1	x 2	x 4

2. **Percentage or Factor Method**

Bond Principle Amt =   Bond Face Amount   x   Bond Issue factor divided by 100

+ Accrued Interest =   Bond Face Amount   x   Bond - Interest Rate   x Time

Bond Issue Price   (From Date of bond
                                                                                       to Bond issue date)

Example: *Bond dated 1/1. Bond Issued 3/1. 800, $1,000 Bonds were issued at 10% to yield 12% for 3 years*

Interest paid: annual—December 30
Interest paid: semiannual—June 30, Dec 30
Interest paid: quarterly—March 30, June 30, September 30, December 30

Interest is Paid	*Annual*	*Semiannual*	*Quarterly*
Stated rate	*10%*	*5.00%*	*2.50%*
Yield rate	*12%*	*6.00%*	*3.00%*
Bond life in years	*3*	*6*	*12*

23

1. Bond Issue price - Present Value (PV) Method

Annual calculation			Calculation	PV-1 12%, 3 periods
Principle	=	569,424	800,000 x 0.71178	PV annuity 12%, 3 periods
+ accrued interest	=	192,151	800,000 x 10% Int. rate x	1 year x 2.40189
Bond Issue Price:	$	761,575	Calculation	PV-1 6% (12% divide by 2), 6 periods (3 yrs times 2)
Semiannual calculation			800,000 x 0.70496	PV annuity 6%, 6 periods
			800,000 x 10% Int. rate x 0.5 year x	4.91732
Principle	=	563,968		
+ Accrued Interest	=	196,693		
Bond Issue Price:	$	760,661	Calculation	PV-1 3% (12% divide by 4), 12 periods (3 years Times 4)
Bond Issue Price:	**$**	**760,184**	800,000 x 0.70138	PV annuity 3%, 12 periods
Quarterly calculation			800,000 x 10% Int. rate x	0.25 year x 9.954
Principle	=	561,104		
+ Accrued Interest	=	199,080		

2. Bond Issue price—Precentage Factor (%'age) Method

Example: Bond dated 1/1. Bond Issued 3/1. 800, $1,000 Bonds were issued at 98 with a 10% rate to yield 12% for 3 years

			Bond Face Amt		Factor or %'age	
Principle	=	784,000 =	800,000	x	98%	= 98 / 100

		Bond Face Amount		Bond Stated Rate	Two (2) months from bond date to bond issue
+ Accrued Interest = 13,333 =		800,000	x	10%	x 2/12 months

Bond Issue Price: $ 797,333

Determine Bond Discount or Premium

Bond amount	$ 800,000
- Bond issue price	- 797,333
Bond discount	**$ 2,667**

Example I:

Bond dated 1/1. Bond Issued 3/1. 800, $1,000 bonds were issued at 10% rate to yield 12% for 3 years

Interest paid—Annual	December 30
Interest paid—Semiannual	June 30, Dec 30
Interest paid quarterly	March 30, June 30, September 30, December 30

Interest is Paid	Annual	Semiannual	Quarterly
Stated rate	10%	5.00%	2.50%
Yield rate	12%	6.00%	3.00%
Bond Life - years	3	6	12

Bond Discount or Premium Determination

Annual calculation

Principle		800,000
- Bond issue price	$	(761,575)
Bond - discount	**$**	**38,425** Face amount (principle) > bond issue price

Semiannual calculation

Principle		800,000
- Bond issue price	$	(760,661)
Bond - discount	**$**	**39,339** Face amount (principle) > bond issue Price

Quarterly calculation

Principle		800,000
- Bond issue price	$	- (760,184)
Bond – discount	**$**	**39,816** Face Amount (Principle) > Bond Issue Price

Example:

Bond date 1/1. Issue date: 4/1. Issued (500) $1000, 10-year bond at 6% interest payable semiannually to yield 9%.

Semiannually (6/30 and 12/31)—due at the end of the period (ordinary due).

Periods: 10 years x 2		*= 20 periods*	
Stated rate:	*6%*	*x 1/2*	*= 3%*
Market rate:	*9%*	*x 1/2*	*= 4.5%*

Determine the Bond Issue Price Using the Present Value Method

Face amount x PV of $1 at Market rate =   Principal
+ Accrued interest x PV at Market Rate =   + Accrued Interest
Bond issue price   Bond issue price

$500,000 x .41464 PV factor   = $207,320 Principal
+ $500,000 x 3% x 13.00794 PV factor   =   + 195,119 Accrued Interest
                                                                        $402,439 Bond issue price

Determine the Bond Discount

	Face amount	$ 500,000
Less:	Bond issue price	- 402,439
	Bond discount	$ 97,561

Determine Bond Issue Price per Bond

Bond issue price
_____ = Bond issue price per bond
# of bonds issued

$\frac{\$402,439}{500}$ = $805 per bond

Recording the Bond Sale at a Discount

Issuer (Seller)		**Purchaser (Investor)**	
Cash	$402,439	Investment—Bond	$500,000
Discount—BP	97,561	Discount—BP	97,561
BP	$500,000	Cash	$402,439

Example:

Bond date: 1/1. Issue Date: 4/1. Issued (500) $1000, 10-year Bond at 10% semiannually for 101½ yielding 8%.

Determine the Bond Issue Price Using the Effective Interest Method

Face Amount x Discount or premium rate	=	Principal
+ Face amount x Stated rate x Time	= +	Accrued Interest
Bond issue price		Bond issue price

Example:

$500,000 x	101.5/100	= $507,500 Principal	Jan. 1 to Mar. 31 = 3 months
$500,000 x	10% x 3/12	= 12,500 Accrued interest (from date of bond to issue date)	
		$520,000 Bond issue price	

Determine the Bond Premium

	Face amount	$500,000
Less:	Bond issue price	- 520,000
	Bond premium	$ 20,000

Determine the Bond Issue Price per Bond

Bond issue price

_____ = Bond issue price per bond

Quantity of bonds issued

$$\frac{\$520,000}{500} = \$1,040$$

Record Bond Issue at a Premium

Issuer (Seller)		**Purchaser (Investor)**	
Cash	$520,000	Investment in bond	$500,000
Premium—BP	20,000	Premium—BP	20,000
Bond Payable (BP)	$500,000	Cash	$520,000

Amortize Bond Discount Using the Effective Interest Method

Example:

Bond date: 1/1. Issued date: 4/1. (500) $1,000 10-year bonds at 6% semiannually yielding 9%.

Calculate Bond Discount Amortization Expense Using Effective Interest Method

Book value of bond x Yield x Time   = Interest expense or revenue

Less: <u>Face amount x Stated x Time = Interest payable or receivable</u>

Amortized discount

$402,439 x 9% x 6/12 = $18,110 Interest expense or revenue

Less: <u>$500,000 x 6% x 6/12 = - 15,000 Interest payable or receivable</u>

$ 3,110 Amortized discount

Overview of Bond Amortization—Discount—Effective Interest Method

	Interest Expense **4.5%**	minus	Interest Payable **3%**		Discount Amortized	Discount Unamortized	BV of Bond
7/1						$97,561	$402,439
12/31	$18,110	—	15,000	=	3,110	94,451	405,549
6/30	$18,250	—	15,000	=	3,250	91,201	408,799
12/31	$18,396	—	15,000	=	3,396	87,805	412,195

Record Amortization of Bond Discount

Issuer (Seller)		**Purchaser (Investor)**	
Interest expense	$18,110	Interest receivable	$15,000
Discount—BP	3,110	Discount—BP	3,110
Interest payable	$15,000	Interest income	$18,110

Description	**Activity**
Interest expense:	Increases over time.
Amortized discount:	Increases over time.
Unamortized discount balance:	Decreases over time.
Bond book value:	Increases over time.

Amortization of Bond Premium

Example:

Bond date: 1/1. Issue date: 4/1. Issued (500) $1000, 10-year bond at 10% semiannually for 101½ yielding 8%.

Calculate Bond Premium Amortization Expense Using the Effective Interest Method

Book value of bond x Yield x Time = Interest expense or revenue

Less: <u>Face amount x Stated x Time = Interest payable or receivable</u>

Amortized premium

$520,000 x 8% x 6/12   = $20,800 Interest expense or revenue

Less: $500,000 x 10% x 6/12=- 25,000 Interest payable or receivable

$ 4,200 Amortized premium

Overview of Bond Premium—Effective Interest Method

	Interest Expense **4%** minus		Interest Payable **5%**	Premium Amortized	Premium Unamortized Bal.	BV of Bond
7/1					$20,000	$520,000
12/31	$20,800	-	25,000	4,200	15,800	515,800
6/30	20,632	-	25,000	4,368	11,432	511,432
12/31	20,457	-	25,000	4,542	6,889	$506,890

Record Amortized Bond Premium

Issuer (Seller)

Interest expense	$20,800
Premium on bond payable	4,200
Interest payable	$25,000

Purchaser (Investor)

Interest Receivable $	25,000
Premium on bond payable	4,200
Interest income	$20,800

Description	Activity
Interest expense:	Decreases over time.
Premium amortized:	Increases over time.
Premium unamortized balance:	Decreases over time.
Book value (BV) of bond:	Decreases over time.

Amortization of Bond Discount Using the Straight Line method

Example:

Bond date: 1/1. Issued date: 4/1. (500) $1,000 10-year bonds at 6% semiannually yielding 9%.

Overview of Bond Discount Amortization Using the Straight Line Method

	Interest Expense **4.5%** minus		Interest Payable **3%**	Discount Amortized		Discount Unamortized Bal.	BV of Bond
7/1						$97,561	$402,439
12/31	$19,878	-	15,000	4,878	=	92,683	407,317
6/30	$19,878	-	15,000	4,878	=	87,805	412,195
12/31	$19,878	-	15,000	4,878	=	82,927	$417,073

Calculate Amortization of Bond Discount Using the Straight Line Method

$\underline{\text{Unamortized bond discount}}$ $\underline{\$97,561}$ = $813 monthly amortized discount

Life of bond from date of bond   120 months

Amortized discount $813 x 6 months   = $4,878 Amortized discount
(Semiannual interest period)

Amortized discount $4,878 + Interest payable $15,000 = Interest expense $19,878
($500,000 x 6% x 1/2)

Record Amortized Bond Discount

Issuer (Seller)

Interest Expense	$19,878
Discount Bond Payable	4,878
Interest Payable	$15,000

Purchaser (Investor)

Interest Receivable	$15,000
Discount Bond Payable	4,878
Interest Income	$19,878

Description	Activity
Interest expense:	Unchanged over time.
Discount amortized:	Unchanged over time.
Discount unamortized balance:	Decreases over time.
Book value (BV) of bond:	Increases over time.

Amortization of Bond Premium Using the Straight Line Method

Example:

Bond date: 1/1. Issue date: 4/1. Issued (500) $1000, 10-year Bond at 10% semiannually for 101½ yielding 8%.

Overview of Bond Premium Amortization Using the Straight Line Method

	Interest Expense @ **4%** minus	Interest Payable @ **5%** =	Premium Amortized	Premium Unamortized Bal.	BV of Bond
7/1				20,000	$520,000
12/31	$24,000	— 25,000	= 1,000	19,000	519,000
6/30	24,000	— 25,000	= 1,000	18,000	518,000
12/31	$24,000	— 25,000	= 1,000	17,000	$517,000

Calculate Amortization of Bond Premium Using the Straight Line Method

$\underline{\text{Unamortized bond premium}}$ $\underline{\$20,000}$ = $167 monthly Amortized Premium

Life of bond from date of bond   120 months

Amortized premium $167 x 6 months   = $1,000 Amortized premium
(Semiannual interest period)

Amortized premium $1,000 minus Interest payable $25,000 = Interest expense $24,000
($500,000 x 10% x 1/2)

Record Amortized Bond Premium

Issuer (Seller)   **Purchaser (Investor)**

Interest expense	$24,000	Interest Receivable	$25,000
Premium on bond payable	1,000	Premium on Bond Payable	1,000
Interest payable	$25,000	Interest income	$24,000

Description	Activity
Interest expense:	Unchanged over time.
Premium amortized:	Unchanged over time.
Premium unamortized balance:	Decreases over time.
Bond book value:	Decreases over time.

Overview of Methods

Discount	Straight Line	vs.	Effective Interest
Interest expense:	SL	>	Effective
Amortized discount:	SL	>	Effective
Unamortized balance:	SL	<	Effective
Bond book value:	SL	>	Effective

Overview of a Bond Amortization Schedule—Discount—Straight Line Method

	Interest Expense		Interest minus Payable	=	Discount	Amortized Discount	Unamortized BV of Bond
7/1						$97,561	$402,439
12/31	$19,878	-	15,000	=	4,878	92,683	407,317
6/30	19,878	-	15,000	=	4,878	87,805	412,195
12/31	19,878	-	15,000	=	4,878	82,927	$417,073

Overview of Bond Amortization Schedule—Discount—Effective Interest Method

	Interest Expense	minus Payable =	Amortized Discount	Unamortized Discount	BV of Bond
7/1				$97,561	$402,439
12/31	$18,110	— 15,000 =	3,110	94,451	405,549
6/30	18,250	— 15,000 =	3,250	91,201	408,799
12/31	18,396	— 15,000 =	3,396	87,805	412,195

Overview of Methods

Premium	Straight Line	vs.	Effective Interest
Interest expense:	SL	>	Effective
Amortized premium:	SL	<	Effective
Unamortized balance:	SL	>	Effective
Bond book value:	SL	>	Effective

Overview of a Bond Amortization Schedule—Premium—Straight Line Method

	Interest Expense	minus Payable =	Amortized Premium	Unamortized Premium	BV of Bond
7/1				20,000	$520,000
12/31	$24,000	— 25,000 =	1,000	19,000	519,000
6/30	24,000	— 25,000 =	1,000	18,000	518,000
12/31	24,000	— 25,000 =	1,000	17,000	517,000

Overview of Bond Amortization Schedule—Premium—Effective Interest Method

	Interest Expense	minus Payable =	Amortized Premium	Unamortized Premium	BV of Bond
7/1				$20,000	$520,000
12/31	$20,800	- 25,000 =	4,200	15,800	515,800
6/30	20,632	- 25,000 =	4,368	11,432	511,432
12/31	$20,457	- 25,000 =	4,542	6,889	$506,889

Fair Value (FV) Method Elected
1. Fair value method is not required.
2. Fair value method may be elected.
3. The election is made at origination date.
4. Once elected it cannot be changed.
5. No bond discount or premium is recorded.
6. Bond is recorded at net of discount or premium.
7. Book value (BV) of the bond is adjusted to fair value.
8. Unrealized gains or losses are recognized in the income statement; gain or loss is recognized as the difference between fair value and book value.
9. Amortize the bond using effective interest method or use a different method if preferred.

Seller (Issuer)

Recognizes an unrealized gain or loss.

FV - Bond >   BV - Bond = Loss Recognized
FV - Bond <   BV - Bond = Gain Recognized

Purchaser (Buyer)

Recognizes an unrealized gain or loss.

FV - Bond >   BV - Bond = Gain recognized
FV - Bond <   BV - Bond = Loss recognized

Example:

Seller

		Bd at Discount	*Bd at Discount*
	FV—Bond	**$785,000**	**$755,000**
Minus	BV—Bond	-760,000	-760,000
	Gain/(Loss) Recognized	**$-25,000**	**$ 5,000**

If, fair value > book value = Loss

Loss—Bond $25,000   *Seller would pay more (FV) than owed (BV).*
   Bond payable   25,000

If, fair value < book balue = Gain

Bond payable $5,000   *Seller would pay less (FV) than owed (BV).*
   Gain—Bond   5,000

Example:

Purchaser

		Bd at Discount	Bd at Discount
	FV—Bond	$785,000	$755,000
Minus	BV—Bond	-760,000	-760,000
	Gain/(Loss) Recog.	$ 25,000	$ -5,000

If fair value > book value = Gain

Investment bond $25,000   *Buyer would receive more (FV) than owed (BV).*

    Gain bond   25,000

If fair value < book value = Loss

Loss bond $5,000   *Seller would receive less (FV) than owed (BV).*

    Investment bond   5,000

Example:

Seller

		Bd at premium	Bd at premium
	FV—Bond	$1,020,000	$ 785,000
Minus	BV—Bond	-1,010,000	-1,010,000
	Gain/(Loss) Recognized	$-10,000	$ 225,000

If fair value > book value = Loss

Loss bond $10,000   *Seller would pay more (FV) than owed (BV).*

    Bond payable   10,000

If fair value < book value = Gain

Bond payable $225,000   *Seller would pay less (FV) than owed (BV).*

    Gain bond   225,000

Example:

Purchaser

		Bd at Premium	**Bd at Premium**
	FV—Bond	**$1,020,000**	**$785,000**
Minus	*BV—Bond*	-1,010,000	-1,010,000
	Gain/(Loss) Recog.	**$ 10,000**	**$-225,000**

If fair value > book value = Gain

Investment bond	$10,000		Buyer would receive more (FV) than owed (BV).
Gain bond		10,000	

If fair value < book value = Loss

Loss bond	$225,000		Seller would receive less (FV) than owed (BV).
Investment bond		225,000	

Bond Redemption

Issuer redeems (redemption price) bond from purchaser.

Seller (issuer redeems bond):   If seller pays > owed = Loss on redemption for seller.

Buyer (purchaser):   Receives > owed = Gain on redemption for buyer.

Seller (Issuer)

Redemption price (paid)	>	BV- Bond (owed) = Loss – Bond redemption
Redemption price (paid)	<	BV- Bond (owed) = Gain – Bond redemption

Purchaser (Buyer)

Redemption price (received)	>	BV- Bond (owed) = Gain – Bond redemption
Redemption price (received)	<	BV- Bond (owed) = Loss – Bond redemption

Example:

Redeemed all outstanding bonds for $825,000.
1/1 Year 1 $800,000 - 10 yr Convertible Bonds were issued at 7% to yield 10%. Interest is paid annually on 12/31.
1/1 Year 4 The bonds had not been converted. The book value of bonds at date of redemption is <u>$671,960.</u>

Redemption price	825,000
Bond Payable	800,000
Book Value bond	671,960
Unamortized Bd issue Cost	0

Record Bond Redemption - Issuer

Loss— Bond Redemption   153,040

BP	800,000	
Disc - BP	128,040	} 671,960 = BV - Bond
Cash	825,000	
Bond issue cost	0	

Redeemer paid > Owed = Loss is recorded.

Record Bond Redemption - Purchaser

Buyer received > Owed = Gain is recorded.

Cash	825,000	
Investment in bonds	671,960	
Gain - Bond Redemption	153,040	

Bond Redemption

Gain or Loss (G/L) Recognition on Bond Redemption

Redemption price
Less: <u>Book value of the bond</u>
   G/L Bond redemption
+   <u>Unamortized bond issue cost</u>
   Net G/L—Bond redemption

Example:
Record bond issued at 98 (Discount)

Cash $490   *= ($500 x 98/100)*
*   Disc—BP 10*
*   BP $500*

Record bond redemption at 102 (Premium)

Loss—Bond redemption	***$35***	
Bond Payable	*500*	
* Disc - BP*		*$ 10*
* Cash*		*510 = ($500 x 102/100)*
* Unamortized bond issue cost*		*15*

510   490 =   - 20   minus   15
Paid > Owe = **Loss on bond redemption** *less unamortized bond issue cost*

If

A Bond Issued at a discount and redeemed at a premium = a loss on bond redemption is recognized.

Stated < Yield		:		*Stated > Yield*		*The yield decreased.*
$15	*20*			*$15*	*10*	

Example:

Record Bond Issued at 102 (Premium)

Cash	*$510*		*= ($500 x 102/100)*
	Premium—BP 10		
	BP	*$500*	

Record Bond Redemption *at 98 (Discount)*

Premium - BP	*$ 10*	
Bond payable	*500*	
Gain—Bond Redemption	***$ 5***	
Cash	*490*	*= ($500 x 98/100)*
Unamortized bond issue cost	*15*	

490	*510*	*=*	*20*		*minus*	*15*

Paid > Owe = ***Gain on bond redemption*** *less unamortized bond issue cost*

If

A bond issue at a premium and redeemed at a discount = a gain on bond redemption is recognized.

Stated > Yield		:		*Stated < Yield*		*The yield increased.*
$15	*10*			*$15*	*20*	

Convertible Bond

Convertible bonds are usually unsecured bonds that can be converted to common or preferred stock within a certain period of time at the discretion of the investor as stated in the bond agreement.

Two Methods of Bond Conversion

1. Book value (BV) method
   a. Reclassify BV of bond to equity.
   b. No gain/loss recognized.

2. Fair value (FV) method
   a. Reclassify BV of bond to equity.
   b. Gain/loss recognized.

1. **Book Value (BV) Method**	2. **Fair Value (FV) Method**
Reclassify the BV of the bond (investment in bonds) to investment in stock	Reclassify the BV of the bond (investment in bonds) to investment in stock. And, recognize gain or loss.
Seller (Issuer) / Purchaser (Buyer)	**Purchaser (Buyer)**
Book Value (BV) Method	**Fair Value (FV) Method**
Bond - Book Value (BV) Par Value - Stock <u>-Unamortized - Bd Issue Cost</u> **APIC**	FMV - Stock <u>- Bond Book Value (BV)</u> **G/L Recog. Bond Conversion**
	Seller (Issuer)
	Fair Value (FV) Method
	FMV - stock share <u>- Par Value - stock share</u> **APIC per share** x # of Stk shares = **APIC**
	FMV - stock - Bond Book Value (BV) - Unamortized - Bd Issue Cost - Par Value - stock <u>- APIC</u> **G/L Recognized bond conversion**

Book Value Method (GAAP)
Bondholder is a purchaser of a bond.
The holder of a convertible bond has the option to convert the bonds into common or preferred stock. This is a debt to equity conversion.
- The long-term debt (bond) is converted into common stock at the option of the holder.
- The liability is transferred to stockholders' equity.
- No gain or loss is recognized on bond conversion.

Example:
Bond holder purchased (500) $1,000 10-year bonds at 7% to yield 9%, interest paid annually, and immediately converted them into 50,000 common stock shares at $1 par value. Unamortized bond issue cost at date of conversion was $11,600. Market value of stock on date of conversion is $465,000.

$500,000 x .42241 =	$211,205		Face amount	$500,000
500,000 x 7% x 6.41766 =	+ 224,618		BV—Bond	- 435,823
Book value (BV) **of bond $**	**435,823**		**Bond Discount:**	**$ 64,177**

Bond holder purchased (500) $1,000 10 yr. bonds at 9% to yield 7%, interest paid annually, and immediately converted into 50,000 common stock shares at $1 par value. Unamortized bond issue cost at date of conversion was $11,600. Market value of stock on date of conversion is $566,500.

$500,000 x .50835 =	$254,175		*Face Amt*	$500,000
500,000 x 9% x 7.02358 =	+ 316,061		*BV—Bond*	- 570,236
Book value *(BV)* **of bond**	**$570,236**		**Bond primium: $ 70,236**	

			Discount	*Premium*
	BV—Bond		$435,823	$570,236
Less:	Par value—CS		—50,000	—50,000
Less:	Unamortized bond issue cost		—11,600	—11,600
	APIC—CS		$374,223	$508,636

Record the Bond Conversion:

When issued at a discount

BP	$500,000	
Disc—BP		64,177
CS		50,000
APIC—CS		374,223
Unamortized bond issue cost		11,600

When issued at a premium

BP	$500,000	
Prem—BP	70,236	
CS		50,000
APIC—CS		508,636
Unamortized bond issue cost		11,600

Fair Market Value Method (Not GAAP)

Bondholder is a purchaser of a bond.

The holder of a convertible bond has the option to convert the bonds into common or preferred stock. This is a debt to equity conversion.

- The long-term debt (bond) is converted into common stock at the option of the holder.
- The liability is transferred to stockholders' equity.
- Gain or loss is recognized.

Memory Tip: Did you pay > owe?

- If market value of stock > book value of bond = loss on bond redemption. Indicates you paid (market value) more than you owe (book value).
- If market value of stock < book value of bond = gain on bond redemption. Indicates you paid (market value) less than you owe (book value).

Example:

Bond holder purchased (500) $1,000 10-year bonds at 7% to yield 9%, interest paid annually, and immediately converted them into 50,000 common stock shares at $1 par value. Unamortized bond issue cost at date of conversion was $11,600. Market value of stock on date of conversion is $465,000.

Bond holder purchased (500) $1,000 10-year bonds at 9% to yield 7%, interest paid annually, and immediately converted them into 50,000 common stock shares at $1 par value. Unamortized bond issue cost at date of conversion was $11,600. Market value of stock on date of conversion is $566,500.

Determine G/L Recognized

		Discount	**Premium**
	Book value of bond	$435,823	$570,236
Less:	Market value—stock	—465,000	—580,000
Less:	Unamortized bond issue cost	—11,600	—11,600
	Net G/L recognized	$17,577 Gain	$—21,364 Loss

Determine APIC

		Discount	**Premium**
Market value—stock		$465,000	$580,000
Less:	Par value—stock	—50,000	—50.000
APIC—stock		$415,000	$530,000

Record Bond Conversion

Discount			or	**Premium**	
BP	$500,000			Loss on bond conversion	$ 21,364
Disc—BP	64,177			BP	500,000
CS	50,000			Premium—BP	70,236
APIC—CS	415,000			CS	50,000
Bond issue cost unamortized	11,600			APIC—CS	530,000
Gain on bond conversion	17,577			Bond issue cost unamortized	11,600

Bond Issued with Detachable Warrants

A detachable warrant is a derivative instrument attached to a bond that gives the purchaser the right to purchase a security (underlying) at a specific price (exercise price) within a certain period of time (exercise period).

The underlying can later be sold separately from the bond.

Determine Stock Warrant Value

	Quantity of Warrants Issued	x	Fair value (FV) per Warrant	=	**Stock Warrant $ value**
Disount:	50,000	x	$1.50	=	**$75,000**
Premium:	50,000	x	$1.10	=	**$55,000**

Determine Bond Issue Price

	Discount	Premium
Bond issue price with warrants	$530,000	$575,000
Less: <u>Stock warrant value</u>	- 75,000	- 55,000
Bond issue price	**$455,000**	**$520,000**
Less: <u>Bond Face Amount</u>	- 500,000	- 500,000
Bond (discount) or **premium**	$ 45,000	$ 20,000

Bond Issuer (Seller)

	Discount			Premium	
Cash	$530,000		Cash		$575,000
Bd-Disc.	45,000		Bond payable		500,000
Bd payable		500,000	Bd-Prem.		20,000
PIC—Stk Warrant		75,000	PIC—Stk Warrant		55,000

Warrants are exercised

	Discount			Premium	
Cash	65,000		Cash	65,000	
PIC—Stk Warrant	75,000		PIC—Stk Warrant	55,000	
CS		50,000	CS		50,000
APIC		90,000	APIC		70,000

Purchaser (Buyer)

Record Bond Issue with Warrants			**Record Warrants Exercised**		
Investment—bond	$455,000		Investment—stock	$140,000	
Investment—warrant	75,000		Investment—warrant		75,000
Cash		530,000	Cash		65,000

Investment—bond	$520,000		Investment—stock	$120,000	
Investment—warrant	55,000		Investment—warrant		55,000
Cash		575,000	Cash		65,000

Bond with Detachable Warrants

Isolate the value of warrants from bond issue price. Value of the warrants = FMV

Bond issue with Detachable Warrants

Example:
1/1 Yr 1 *Bond issue 800, 10 years $1,000 bonds with detachable stock warrants at 105. Interest paid annually - 12/31.*

10 warrants were issued for each bond.
The FMV of the warrants at date of issue was $3.00.

Bond issue factor		105
Number of warrants per bond.		10
Common stock par value	$	5.00
Exercise price	$	10.00
FV - Warrants	$	3.00

					= 105 / 100
			Number of Bonds	Bond Value	Bond Factor
Issue Price	$840,000	=	800	$1,000	**$1.05**
			Number of Warrants	Quantity of Bond s	FMV of Warrants
Less: Value of warrants	(24,000)	=	10	(800)	**$3.00**
Bond - BV	**$816,000**				
Less: Bond payable (BP)	(800,000)				
Bond Premium–unamortized:	**$16,000**				

Bond Issuer (Seller)

Record Bond Issue with Stock Warrants   Number of Warrants Quantity of Bond s   Bond Issue Price

Cash	840,000	10	(800)	105 divided by 100
BP	800,000			
BP - Premium	16,000			
PIC - Stock warrants	24,000			

Record Stock Warrants Exercised

Cash	80,000	
PIC - Stock warrants	24,000	
CS		40,000
APIC		64,000 = plug to balance entry.

	Cash Received		Number of Warrants Per Bond	Number of Bonds Issued	Exercise Price
Cash	80,000	=	10 x	800	x $10

	CS par value $ amount		# of warrants per bond	# of bonds issued	CS par value
CS	40,000	=	10 x	800	x $5

Bond Purchaser (Investor, Holder, Owner)

Record Bond Issue with Stock Warrants

Investment in Bonds	816,000	
Investment in Stock Warrants	24,000	
Cash		840,000

Record Stock Warrants Exercised

Investment in Stock	104,000	
Investment in Stock Warrants		24,000
Cash		80,000

	Cash paid		Number of Warrants Per Bond	Number of Bonds Issued	Exercise Price
Cash	80,000	=	10 x	800	x $10

Bond with Detachable Warrants
Isolate the value of warrants from bond issue price. Value of the warrants = FMV

Bond issue with Detachable Warrants
Example:
1/1 Yr 1 Bond issue 800, 10 years $1,000 bonds with detachable stock warrants at 105.
Interest paid annually - 12/31. Ten (10) warrants were issued for each bond. The FMV of the warrants at date of issue was $3.00.

Bond issue factor	105
# of warrants per bond.	10
CS par value	$ 5.00
Exercise price	$ 10.00
FV—warrants	$ 3.00

			Number of Warrants	Quantity of Bonds	FMV of warrants
Issue Price	$840,000				
Less: _Value of Warrants_	(24,000)	=	10 x	(800) x	**$3.00**
Bond book value	**$816,000**				
Less: _Bond payable (BP)_	(800,000)				
Bond Premium unamortized:	**$16,000**				

		Number of Bonds	Bond Value	105 / 100 Bond Factor
$840,000	=	800 x	$1,000 x	**$1.05**
($24,000)	=	Number of warrants 10 x	Quantity of bonds x (800)	FMV of Warrants **$3.00**

Bond Issuer (Seller)

Record Bond Issue w/ Stk Warrants	Number of warrants	Quantity of Bonds	Bond Issue Price
Cash 840,000	10 x	(800) x	105 divided by 100
BP 800,000			
BP—Premium 16,000			
PIC—Stock warrants 24,000			

Record Stock Warrants Exercised

Cash	80,000	
PIC—Stock warrants	24,000	
Common stock:		40,000
APIC		64,000 = Plug to balance entry.

	Cash Received		Number of Warrants Per Bond		Number of bonds Issued		Exercise Price
Cash	80,000	=	10	x	800	x	$10
CS	40,000	=	10	x	800	x	$5

Bond Purchaser (Investor, Holder, Owner)

Record Bond Issue with Stock Warrants

Investment in bonds	816,000
Investment in stock warrants	24,000
Cash	840,000

Record Stock Warrants Exercised

Investment in stock	104,000
Investment in stock warrants	24,000
Cash	80,000

	Cash Paid		**# of Warrants**		**# of Bonds Issued**		**Exercise Price**
Cash	80,000	=	10	x	800	x	$10

BUSINESS COMBINATIONS

Business Combinations
- SFAS 141—Accounting for business combinations
- ASC 805—Business combinations

- Purchase transaction
    - Investor or acquirer
        - Acquires a controlling ownership interest ≥ 50% in investee (acquiree)
        - Acquisition cost associated with the purchase is expensed.
            - Example
                - Consultant fees to arrange acquisition.
                - Accounting and legal fees associated with the valuation and acquisition process.
                - Commissions are expensed.
        - Cost of registering and issuing stock is applied against the stock issue.
        - Consolidated Financial Statements (FS)
            - Accounting Research Bulletin (ARB) 51 requires all entities to prepare consolidated financial statements for entities in which it has a controlling interest.
            - Economic entity
                - In form—separate legal entity
                - In substance—legal entities are one
        - Combined financial statements (FS)
            - Several corporations
            - Under common management in which one has a controlling interest.
- A business combination
    - Merger   A + B = A
        - Assets and liabilities are acquired in exchange for cash, stock or debt securities.
        - The acquired company ceases to exist; the books are closed.
        - Assets and liabilities are recorded on the Investor's (purchaser's) books.
- Acquisition   A + B = AB
    - One corporation acquires a controlling interest of another corporation.
    - The acquired company continues to operate as a separate legal entity.
    - Assets and liabilities are recorded on the investor's (purchaser's) combined or consolidated financial statements.
- Consolidation   A + B = C
    - An acquisition.
    - The acquired company continues to operate as a separate legal company.
    - Company C is formed as the combined unit of A and B.

Overview

1) Determine at date of acquisition.
    a) Fair value (FV) of acquiree.
    b) FV noncontrolling interest.
    c) Goodwill (GW) or bargain purchase gain.
    d) Record purchase.

2) Record period activity.
3) Record eliminating journal entries (EJE).
4) Consolidate financial statements (FS)

1) **Acquirer**
   a) Acquires a controlling interest: > 50% ownership interest in acquired entity which gives the acaqirer
      (1) Controlling interest.
      (2) Significant influence over the entity.
      (3) The right to vote on corporate policy.
2) **Determine fair value (FV) of acquiree at the date of acquisition**

   Assets
   Less: <u>Liabilities</u>
   Net assets at book value (BV)
   + <u>FV adjustment (valuation allowance)</u>
   Net assets at fair value (FV)

Determine the book value of assets and liabilities determine the fair value of assets and liabilities

- Use investee's most recent audited FS.
- Request detail schedule of assets and liabilities

- Appraised value (investor's request)
- Net realized value
- Selling price less cost of disposal

3) **Determine noncontrolling interest at the date of acquisition**
   a) Noncontrolling interest is sometimes referred to as minority interest.
   b) Financial Accounting Standard Board (FASB) 160 sets the standard for noncontrolling interest in consolidated financial statements.
   c) Noncontrolling Interest is a long-term liability.
   d) And, is a 3rd party's ownership interest < 50% in Investee.

   100% Ownership interest
   Less: <u>Purchased ownership %'age</u>
   Noncontrolling interest %'age

Noncontrolling interest $ amount = Noncontrolling interest percentage **times** fair value—acquiree

4) **Determine goodwill (GW) at the date of acquisition**

   Noncontrolling interest at FV
   Purchase price of acquiree
   Less: <u>Acquiree net assets at FV</u>
   Goodwill

Goodwill = Noncontrolling interest + Purchase price of acquiree > Acquiree net assets at FV

5) **Determine gain—bargain purchase at the date of acquisition, if applicable.**

   Noncontrolling interest at FV
   Purchase price of acquiree
   Less: <u>Acquiree net assets at FV</u>
   Gain—Bargain purchase

Gain from bargain purchase = Noncontrolling interest + Purchase price of acquiree < Acquiree net assets at FV

6) **Record purchase at the date of acquisition**
   a) Cash purchase

Investment in company	$$$
Cash	$$$

   b) Stock issue to purchase acquiree

Investment in company	$$$	at purchase price
CS	$$$	at par
APIC	$$$	plug value

Example:

7/1/ Year Company A paid $500k to acquire 80% of Company B (acquiree).

Determine the fair value of Company B at date of acquisition

Assets	$862.50
Less: Liabilities	- 300.00
Net assets at book value	**562.50**
+ FV adjustment—inventory	10.00
FV Adjustment—PP&E	27.50
Net assets at fair value	**$600.00**

Determine the BV of assets and liabilities
- Use investee's most recent audited FS.
- Request detail schedule of assets and liabilities

Determine the FV of assets and liabilities
- Appraised value (Investor's request)
- Net realized value (NRV)
- Selling price less cost of disposal

Record cash purchase at date of acquisition

Investment in comp B	$500
Cash	$500

Net assets of Company B (acquiree)

CS—common stock	$100.00
APIC—additional paid in capital	250.00
Retained earnings	212.50
Net assets at book value	**$562.50**

Determine Company A's ownership interest in Company B at date of acquisition

	Company A ownership in Company B		Ownership %	
Assets	$ 862.50	=	Assets	$ 690
Less: Liabilities	- 300.00	=	- Liabilities	- 240
Net assets at book value	562.50	x 80% =	Net Assets at BV	450
+FMV valuation adjustment—Inventory	10.00	=	FMV adjustment—Inv	8
FMV valuation adjustment—PP&E	27.50		FMV adjustment PP&E	22
Net assets at fair market value	**$600.00**	=	**Net Assets at FMV $480**	

Accounting for the Fair Value (FV) of Acquiree
Valuation Allowance

- FV valuation adjustment is called valuation allowance; it represent the fair value adjustment to assets and liabilities.
- The fair value adjustment is applied to the book value of all assets and liabilities.
- The fair value adjustment for capital assets is amortized over the remaining life of the asset.

Amortize valuation allowance

Asset FV adjustment	$22.00	=	Amortized expense	$4.40
Remaining life of asset 5 years				

Record amortize valuation allowance

Income from investment	$4.40	
Investment in corporate stock		$4.40

Determine goodwill (GW) at date of acquisition

	Noncontrolling interest at FMV	$120
	Purchase price	500
Less:	FV of acquiree net assets	- 600
	Goodwill	**$ 20**

- Goodwill (GW) is a long-term asset.
- It is *not* amortized.
- It is tested *annually* for impairment.

Impairment test: FV of GW < BV of GW = Impairment loss – GW

$$\$15 \quad < \quad \$20 \quad = \quad \textbf{-\$5.00}$$

Alternate method of estimating impairment value:
GW x Estimated impairment loss % = Impairment loss – GW

Recording Goodwill Impairment

Impairment loss – GW	$5.00
GW	$5.00

Determine Gain—Bargain Purchase at Date of Acquisition, if Applicable

	Noncontrolling interest at FMV	$120
	Purchase price	500
Less:	FV of acquiree net assets	- 675
	Gain—Bargain purchase $	**-55**

"Noncontrolling interest" is the new term used for minority interest (MI).

Determine Noncontrolling Interest (NCI)

100% Ownership interest	
Less: Purchased ownership %'age	
Noncontrolling interest %'age	

Determine Noncontrolling Interest (NCI) in Acquiree at Date of Acquisition

Noncontrolling interest in acquiree			Minority Interest	
Assets	$862.50		Assets	$ 172.50
Less: Liabilities	- 300.00		- Liabilities	- 60.00
Net assets at book value	562.50	x 20% =	Net assets at BV	$112.50
+ FMV Adjustment—Inventory	10.00		FMV Adjustment—Inventory	**2.00**
PP&E	27.50		PP&E at FMV	**5.50**
Net assets at fair market value	**$600.00**		**Net assets at FV**	**$120.00**

Net assets of Company B (acquiree)

Common stock	$100.00	x	20%	= $20.00
Additional paid in capital	250.00	x	20%	= $50.00
Retained earnings	212.50	x	20%	= $42.50
Net assets at book value	**$562.50**			**$112.50**

- Noncontrolling Interest is a Long Term Liability.
- Noncontrolling Interest is a 3rd party's ownership interest < 50% in Investee.

Record Period Activity

Determine Ending Balance of Investment Account (Acquirer's Books)

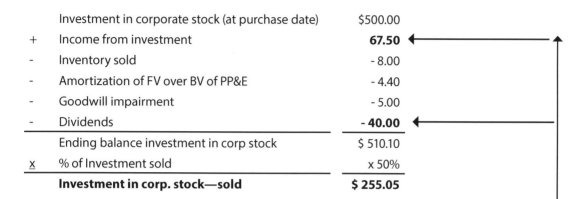

	Investment in corporate stock (at purchase date)	$500.00
+	Income from investment	**67.50**
-	Inventory sold	- 8.00
-	Amortization of FV over BV of PP&E	- 4.40
-	Goodwill impairment	- 5.00
-	Dividends	**- 40.00**
	Ending balance investment in corp stock	$ 510.10
x	% of Investment sold	x 50%
	Investment in corp. stock—sold	**$ 255.05**

Determine Gain or Loss (G/L) on Sale of Investment

	Sale price	$260.00
-	Investment in corporate stock—sold	**- 255.05**
	Capital gain on sale of investment	$ 4.95

Determine Income from Investment

Income from investment is also referred to as equity in earnings.

12/31 Acquiree net Income $180,000.

July–December

$\dfrac{\$180{,}000}{12\ \text{months}}$ = $15,000 x 6 months = $90,000

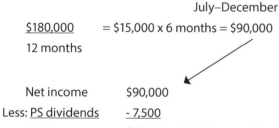

Net income	$90,000	
Less: PS dividends	- 7,500	
Net income	$82,500 x 80% Ownership interest	= $66,000 Equity in earnings
PS dividends	$ 7,500 x 20% Ownership interest	= $ 1,500 Equity in earnings
		$ 67,500 Equity in earnings

Determine dividend distribution

Dividends to investor $50,000 Dividends x 80% = **$40,000**

Dividends to noncontrolling interest $50,000 Dividends x 20% = $10,000

Determine ending balance of noncontrolling interest (NCI) (acquirer's books)

	Beginning NCI	$120.00 = Net assets at FV $600k	x NCI % 20	
	Equity in earnings	18.00 = Net income $90k	x NCI % 20	
Less:	Dividends	- 10.00 = Dividends $50k	x NCI % 20	
	Ending NCI	**$148.00**		

Record investor's purchase of acquiree (investee)

Cash purchase   or   **Common stock issue**

Cash purchase			Common stock issue	
Investment in corporation	$500,000		Investment in corporation	$500,000
Cash		$500,000	CS	200,000
			APIC	300,000

Record investor's income from investment

Investment in corporation	$67,500
Equity in earnings *or* income from investment	$67,500

Record investor's receipt of dividend

Cash	$40,000
Investment in corporation	$40,000

Record valuation allowance (FV adjustment)

Inventory	$ 8,000	
PP&E	22,000	each PP&E item would be specifically adjusted.
Investment in corporation	$30,000	

Record amortization of FV adjustment

Equity in Earnings	$4,400
Investment in Corp	$4,400

Record GW Impairment

Impairment loss – Goodwill	$5,000
Goodwill	$5,000

Record eliminating journal entries (EJE)

Eliminate intercompany (I/C) transactions as part of the consolidation of financial statements.
- Sales and cost of sales
- Income from investment (or equity in earnings)
- Payables vs. receivables: consolidated FS—payables and receivables are eliminated
- Gross profit (GP) in ending Inventory
- GP on sale of assets

- Bond payable vs. bond receivable
  - Balance is adjusted to bond owner's basis.
  - Adjustment is applied against retained earnings.
    - Buyer's basis > owner's basis = decrease to retained earnings.
    - Buyer's basis < owner's basis = increase to retained earnings.
- Interest income vs. interest expense
- Interest payable vs. interest receivable
- Gain/loss on bond retirement
- Gain/loss on sale

Eliminate intercompany sale

Sale	$
Cost of sale	$

Eliminate intercompany payable and receivable

Payable	$
Receivable	$

Eliminate gross profit (GP) in ending inventory

Cost of sale	$
Inventory	$

Eliminate intercompany sale, cost of sale, and gross profit in ending inventory

Sale	$
Cost of sale	$
Inventory	$

Eliminate gain on intercompany sale of asset

Gain on sale	$	Gain on sale	
Asset	$	Difference	
Accumulated	$	Amount related to sale	

Amortize gain on intercompany sale of asset

Accumulated	$
Depreciation expense	$

As Part of the Consolidation of Financial Statements—on Investor's Books

- Eliminate investee stockholders' equity
- Eliminate investment in investee.
- Record noncontrolling interest
- Record goodwill.
- Mnemonic: **REal MAGIC**
  - **R**etained **E**arnings al (REal)
  - **M** I (Noncontrolling Interest)
  - **A** PIC
  - **G** W

- Investment in Investee
- **CS**

Journal Entry—REal MAGIC

CS	$100.00
APIC	250.00
RE	212.50
GW	20.00
Investment in Corp B	$ 500.00
Noncontrolling Int.	82.50

Intercompany Sale of an Asset

Consolidated FS—the asset book value should equal seller's book value as if sale had not occurred.

Seller	Buyer
A. Record sale of asset	A. Record asset purchase
B. Calculate G/L on sale of asset	B. Record depreciation of asset
C. Record amortization of G/L on sale of asset	
D. Eliminate I/C sale	
D. Eliminate GP on sale of asset	

Seller—Intercompany sale of asset for $99.   **Buyer**

(A) Asset at Net Book Value

Cost	$125
Accumulated	—50
NBV	$ 75

(B) Record sale of asset

Cash	$99	
Accumulated	50	
Asset		125
Gain on Sale		$ 24

(B) Record asset purchase

Asset	$99	
Cash		99

(C) Record depreciation expense

Depreciation expense	$33	
Accumulated depreciation		33

(C) Calculate G/L on asset sale

Proceeds	$99
– NBV	—75
Gain	$ 24

Asset	$99	= $33
Remaining useful life	3 years	

(D) Amortize gain or loss on asset sale

Gain on asset sale $\underline{\$24}$ = Amortized gain $8

Remaining useful life   3 years

(E) Record amortization of gain on sale of asset

Accumulated depreciation $8

    Depreciation expense   8

(F) Eliminate I/C sale and gp on sale

Asset $26 (PLUG)

Gain—Sale   24

    Accumulated depreciation   50

Consolidated financial statements		Cross check	
Buyer's Basis	$99	Asset Buyer's Basis	$99
– Accumulated	—33	+ Asset Adjustment	26
NBV	66	**Original Asset Value**	**125**
		Prior Accumulated depreciation	– 50
– Gain add back	– 24	Current depreciation	- 25
Received amortize gain	8		
Asset NBV should be:	**$ 50**	**NBV:**	**$ 50**

The math: The consolidated financial statements for assets acquired in an intercompany transaction should equal the seller's net book value (NBV) amortized.

NBV $\underline{\$75}$ = $25
      3 years remaining

NBV $75
    - $\underline{25}$ Depreciation
    $50

Intercompany (I/C) Sale of Inventory

- Is a sale of Inventory to related party (subsidiary).
  - Is an intercompany transfer of an asset
- Buyer's basis in the inventory should = Seller's basis when reported in the consolidated financial statement.
  - Eliminate— intercompany sale of inventory
  - Eliminate— intercompany cost of sale of Inventory
  - Eliminate—Gross profit (GP) in ending inventory on buyer's books.

Seller

Sold inventory for $50 to related party.

Buyer

Sold ½ of the inventory to a third party for $30.

	Beg. inventory	$ 70
Less:	I/C COS	—40
	Endg inventory	$30

Records Purchase of Inventory for $50

Inventory $50
      Intercompany payable $50

Calculate GP on Sale of Inventory to Subsidiary

Sale	$50	
- COS	—40	
GP	$10	(20% GP)

Record Sale of Inventory to 3rd Party for $30

| Accounts recievable | $30 |
| Sale | 30 |

| COS $25 | |
| Inventory 25 | |

Sold half of inventory for $30.

Seller records sale of inventory to subsidiary

I/C receivable $50
I/C sale 50

I/C COS $40
Inventory 40

Sale	$50	
- COS	—40	
GP	$10	(20% GP)

Eliminate I/C sale of inventory and gross profit on sale

I/C Sale $50	= the sale amount.
I/C COS 45	= Plug
Inventory 5	= E-Inv. of Sub. $25 x 20% GP

Overview of Consolidated Financial Statements

	Parent	Sub	Total	EJE	Consol'd FS	Check should be
Sale	$50	30	80	—50	30	$ 30
– COS	—40	—25	—65	—45	—20	—20
GP	$10	5	15	-5	10	$ 10
B—Inv	$70	50	120	—50	70	$ 70
– COS	—40	—25	—65	—45	—20	—20
E—Inv	$30	25	55	-5	50	$ 50

Consolidated Balance Sheet
- **Common stock** = Parent (Acquirer)
- **Current assets** = Acquirer + Acquiree + Adjustments
- **Long-term assets** = Acquirer + Acquiree + Adjustments
- **Current liabilities** = Acquirer + Acquiree + Adjustments
- **Long-term liabilities** = Acquirer + Acquiree + Adjustments
- **Stockholders' equity** = Acquirer + Noncontrolling interest

Affiliate = A party under direct or indirect association of another but not controlled by it.

Subsidiary = A company with a majority ownership interest in the stock of another (subsidiary) for which it has control.

Control
- The power of another party to directly influence the management and policies of a party through ownership.

Related Party
- FASB 57—Related Party Disclosure
- ASC 805—Related Party Disclsoure
- is under Common Ownership or Management Control
- a Principal Owner with > 10% ownership interest
- Management
  - Board of drectors
  - President
  - Vice president
  - Chief executive officer
  - Chief financial officer
- Immediate family

Related party transaction
- A transaction between companies under common control in the ordinary course of business.
- Excludes
  - Eliminated intercompany transactions
  - Compensation agreements
  - Expense allowance (per diem expenses)
  - Other items in the ordinary course of business.

Related party disclosure
- Financial statements (FS)
  - On the face of the income statement (I/S)
  - On the face of the balance sheet (BS)
- Notes to FS
  - Description—nature of transaction
  - Relationship
  - Amount
  - Terms
- Settlement agreement

Examples—Related Party Transaction

	Financial Statements (FS)	Notes to FS
Employee loans	X	X
Loans—officers	X	X
Due to/from affiliate	X	
Company is a ##		X
Entity under ##		X
Payment to a partnership in which the partner is a manager of the company and a partner in the partnership.		X

CASH FLOW STATEMENT

The cash flow statement reports cash receipts and disbursements during the period from operating, investing, and financing activities.

1. The cash flow statement starts with net income, which is obtained from the current period income statement.
2. The net income is adjusted for monetary and nonmonetary items during the period.
   a. The three cash flow activities are adjusted for monetary and nonmonetary items.
   b. The net change of these three activities are added to the beginning cash and net income for the period.
   c. Beginning cash is obtained from the prior year balance sheet.
3. The result represents the current cash balance for the current period as shown in the current balance sheet.

Three Cash Flow Activities

These are represented in the cash flow statement:

1. **Operating** shows the movement in current assets and liabilities.
2. **Investing** represents the net change in investment purchases and sales for the period.
3. **Financing** shows the movement in liabilities and other activity during the period.

Supplement Information

This reports noncash exchanges of investing and financing activities; for example:

- Debt to equity
- Convertible stock
- Convertible bond

Two(2) Cash flow Formats

These are used to present the statement of cash flow:

- **Direct method** is the preferred method.
  - o Cash receipts and cash disbursement are represented in the three activities.
  - o Noncash transactions are *not* reported.
  - o The reconciliation of net income to net Cash appears at the end of the cash flow statement.
- **Indirect method** is allowed.
  - o Noncash items are eliminated in the three activities.
  - o Changes in assets and liabilities are reported.
    - If the **asset** balance increased from the prior period, deduct the increase from the net income.
    - If the **liability** balance increased from the prior period, add the increase to the net income.
- A reconciliation of net income to net cash appears as part of operating activities.

Two(2) Formats

1. **Direct method**—preferred format. Use this method unless otherwise stated.

        Net Income
        Operating
        Investing
        <u>Financing</u>
        Change in cash
     + <u>Beginning cash</u>
        Ending cash

The reconciliation of net income to net cash from operating activities appears at the end of the cash flow statement and represents noncash activity.

2. **Indirect method**—Allowed

        Net Income
        Reconciliation of net income to net cash from operating activities
        1.   Eliminates noncash activity.
        2.   <u>Reports change in current assets and liabilities</u>
        Net cash from operating activities
        Investing
        <u>Financing</u>
        Change in cash
     + <u>Beginning cash</u>
        Ending cash

1. Cash receipts are (+) added to net income (NI).
2. Cash disbursements are (-) subtracted from NI.

Operating Activities		
Mnemonic:	**GL CALM N DIT**	
		Add or
		Subtract
		to / from **NI**
GL	**G**ains	(-)
	Loss	(+)
CALM	**C**urrent **A**ssets and **L**iabilities **M**onetary items	
C - Current	Changes in **CALM** balance:	
A - Asset	If Current **Asset** balance **increased**, **deduct** from NI	(-)
L - Liability	If Current **Liability** balance **increased**, **add** to NI	(+)
M - Monetary Items	**M**onetary Items	
	Marketable Security	
	Purchase	(-)
	Sale	(+)
	Prepaid	
	Prepaid an expense	(-)
	Income (cash received).	(+)
	Accounts Receivable	
	Cash received	(+)
	Balance increased.	(-)
	Accounts Payable	
	Cash paid	(-)
	Balance increased.	(+)
	Inventory	
	Purchase	(-)
	Balance increased.	(-)
N	**N**onmonetary Items	
	are eliminated:	
	Depreciation	(+)
	Amortization	(+)
	Amortized—bond discount	(+)
	Amortized—bond premium	(-)

	Provision for uncollectible accounts	(+)
	Gain	(-)
	Loss	(+)
	Income from investments (equity in earnings)	(-)
DIT	Cash **D**ividends received, **I**nterest and **T**axes	
D	Cash **D**ividend Received.	(+)
I	**I**nterest	
	Interest	
	Accrued interest expense	(+)
	Accrued interest income	(-)
	Paid interest expense	(-)
	Cash receipt interest income	(+)
T	**T**axes	
	Accrued tax expense	(+)
	Paid taxes	(-)
	Cash receipt tax refund	(+)

1. Cash receipts are (+) added to net income (NI).
2. Cash disbursements are (-) subtracted from NI.

Investing Activities	
Cash purchase	**(+) or (-) to NI**
Property, plant, and equipment	(-)
Investments	(-)
Stocks—equity	(-)
Stocks—debt	(-)
Another company	(-)
Marketable securities	(-)
Bonds (debt security)	(-)
Loans(lending)	(-)
Cash received	**(+)**
Property, plant, and equipment	(+)
Investments	(+)
Stocks—equity	(+)
Stocks—debt	(+)
Another company	(+)
Marketable securities	(+)
Bonds (debt security)	(+)
Loans(laid back)	(+)

Financing Activities		
Debt—long or current portion	**(+) or (-) to NI**	
Bond—sale	(+)	
Bond—purchase		(-)
Note, loan, mortgage		
Principle payment (cash received)	(+)	
Principle payment (cash paid)		(-)
Capital lease		
Principle payment (cash paid)		(-)
Stock		
Issue (sale)— cash receipt	(+)	
Redemption—cash paid		(-)
Cash Dividend—paid		(-)

CHANGES IN ACCOUNTING PRINCIPLES

Accounting Changes
- Change in accounting principle.
  - Prospective approach
  - Retrospective approach
- Change in estimate
- Change in entity

Examples of Accounting Principles

- Depreciation methods—prospective approach
  - Double Declining Balance
  - Straight Line
  - Sum of the Year Digits
  - Units of Production
- Inventory methods—retrospective approach (increased inventory balance)

Last In First Out	Inventory	$$$
First In First Out	Deferred tax liability	$$$
Weighted average	RE	$$$
Single to aggregate approach		

- Long-term contract reporting—retrospective approach (adjusted sales recognition)

Completed	CIP	$$$
Percent complete	Deferred tax liability	$$$
	RE	$$$
Installment		

- Reporting Entity—uses neither prospective or retrospective approach
  - Single entity
  - Combined entity
  - Consolidated entity

Prospective Approach (Indirect Effect)
- The change affects the current and future period.
- Using the new method, apply the change to current and future periods.
- The change is not retroactively applied to the earliest period determined.
- There is no cumulative effect of the change calculated.
  - No restating current year Beginning Retained Earnings.
  - No adjustment to account balances in the current period.
- Financial statements presented on a comparative basis
  - Financial statements re not restated.
  - Financial statements re retrospectively adjusted.

Examples of items using prospective approach:
- Bad debt expense
- Warranty

64

- Useful life
- Salvage value

Retrospective Approach (Direct Effect)

- The change affects the current and prior periods.
- Using the new method, apply the change to current and prior periods.
- The change is retroactively applied to the earliest period determined.
- The cumulative effect of the change is calculated.
- Restate current year beginning retained earnings.
- Adjust account balances in the current period.
- Restate all financial statements presented on a comparative basis.

Examples:

- **Inventory**—retrospective approach (increased inventory balance)

Inventory	$$$	
Deferred Tax Liab		$$$
RE		$$$

- **Long-term contracts**—retrospective approach (adjusted sales recognition)

CIP	$$$	
Deferred tax liability		$$$
RE		$$$

Change in Entity

- Uses a retrospective approach
- Change in reporting entity.
- Restate comparative financial statements presented for all periods.
- Apply the change retroactively to the earliest period that can be determined.

Off-Balance Sheet Loss

- Possible loss from Financial Instrument or Other contracts greater than the amount recognized in the Balance Sheet.

Examples:

- Noncancelable Operating Lessees with future minimum lease payments
- Standby loan commitments
- Letters of credit
- Repurchase agreement

CONTINGENCY

Contingency

- Uses a conservative approach
- Existing condition or subsequent event resulting in an anticipated expense or income.
  - The chance of occurrence is:
    - Likely or probable
    - Reasonably probable
    - Slight or remote
  - The amount can be estimated?
    - Likely or probable
    - Reasonably probable
    - Slight or remote

Contingency—Examples

- Lawsuit (litigation)
- Compensated absences
- Rebates
- Coupons
- Product recall (impairment)
- Product warranty cost (original manufacturer's warranty)
- Casualty
- Guaranteed debt and/or obligations (guaranteeing payment of another's debt)
- Line of credit—obligation
- Repurchase receivable

Recording a Contingency Liability—Example

Estimated lawsuit expense $$$
   Estimated lawsuit liability $$$

Anticipated Expense
- **Probable**
  - Accrue in financial statements
  - Disclose in footnotes the event and $ range.
- **Reasonably probable**
  - Disclose in footnotes the event and $ range.
- **Slight or remote**—No disclosure required.

Anticipated Income
- **Probable**—Accrue in financial statements
  - Disclose in footnotes the event and $ range.
- **Reasonably probable**
  - Disclose in footnotes the event and $ range.
- **Slight or remote**—No disclosure required.

Chance of Occurrence	The $ amount is	Disclosure
Probable	**Known**	**Accrue and disclose in *notes* to FS**
	Estimable	**Accrue and disclose in *notes* to FS**
	Not determinable	No note disclosure or accrual required.
Reasonably Estimable	**Known**	**Disclose in *notes* to FS**
	Estimable	**Disclose in *notes* to FS**
	Not determinable	No note disclosure or accrual required.
Slight or Remote	Known	No note disclosure or accrual required.
	Estimable	No note disclosure or accrual required.
	Not determinable	No note disclosure or accrual required.

CORRECTION OF AN ERROR

Correction of an Error

- **Type of Error**
  - Current period adjustment
    - Self-correcting error
    - Non-self-correcting error
  - Prior period adjustment
    - Self-correcting error
    - Non-self-correcting error
  - Example of errors
    - Misclassified item: item has been classified to the wrong account
    - Non GAAP accounting transaction has been recorded.
    - Non-GAAP to GAAP correcting entry is made.
      - Cash to accrual
      - Gross profit to first in first out, last in first out, or weighted average
    - Failure to record
    - Failure to accrue
    - Over or under accrued
    - Expense capitalized cost.
    - Prepaid revenue is fully recognized.
    - Prepaid expense is fully expensed.

Current Period Adjustment
During the current period, an error has been discovered:
- Current period is *open*: record correcting entry in the current period.
- Current period is *closed*: record correcting entry in the period discovered.

Prior Period Adjustment
During the current period, an error has been discovered in a prior period:
- Prior Period is *open* and prior to the issuance of the financial statements.
  - Posting is allowed to the prior period: record the correcting entry in the prior period.
  - Posting is disallowed: record the correcting entry in the period discovered.
  - Period is *closed* and the financial statements (FS) are issued.
  - Restate the prior period FS for all periods presented.
  - Record the correcting entry in the current period.

Self-Correcting Error (Counterbalancing)
- Error reverses in the subsequent (following) period.
  - Current period is over or under stated.
  - Following period is under or over stated.
    - By the end of the subsequent period the error has corrected itself; YTD balances are properly stated.
- Error discovered during the subsequent (following) period.
  - Record adjusting journal entry (AJE) in current year.
    - Restate beginning retained Earnings (RE) at 1/1.

- Restate prior year (PY) FS.
  - Restate FS for all prior periods presented.
- Footnote disclosure—not required.
- Error discovered beyond self-correcting period
  - No AJE required.
    - By the end of the self-correcting period the error has corrected itself.
  - YTD balances are properly stated.
  - Restate PY FS.
    - Restate FS for all prior periods presented.
  - Footnote disclosure is not required

Self-Correcting Error—Income Statement

	Year 1	Year 2	1/1 Year 3
Revenue	Over ($10)	Under ($10)	Correct
Expense	Under ($5)	Over ($5)	Correct
Net income	Over ($5)	Under ($5)	Correct
Retained earnings	Over ($5)	Correct	Correct

Self Correcting Error—Balance Sheet

	Year 1	Year 2	1/1 Year 3
Asset	Over ($10)	Under ($10)	Correct
Liability	Under ($5)	Over ($5)	Correct
Working capital	Over ($5)	Under ($5)	Correct
Stockholders' equity	Over ($5)	Correct	Correct

Non-Self-Correcting Error (Noncounterbalancing)
- Error is not self-correcting.
  - Record Adjusting journal entry in current period.
  - Restate beginning Retained earnings at 1/1.
  - Restate Prior year financial statement.
    - Restate financial statement for all prior periods presented.
  - Footnote disclosure is not required

Prepaid Expense or Revenue is Fully Recognized
- Retroactive approach
  - Restate the FS for the period effected.
  - Record AJE as of 1/1 current year.
- Examples
  - Expense
  - Revenue

Prepaid Expense

Prepaid expense	$$.$$
Deferred tax liability	$$.$$
Retained earnings	$$.$$

Prepaid Revenue

Deferred tax asset	$$.$$
Retained earnings	$$.$$
Unearned revenue	$$.$$

Fully Expensed Capitalized Cost

- Retroactive approach
    - Restate FS for the period effected.
    - Record AJE as of 1/1 current year.

Asset	$$.$$
Accumulated depreciation	$$.$$
Retained earnings	$$.$$

Effects of Over or Under Stating— Inventory

Inventory Under/Over	Beg	COS	NI	RE	Self-Correcting After 2 years
Beg—Inv. Under	Okay	Under	Over	Okay	Y
End—Inventory under	Under	Over	Under	Under	Y
Begginning— Inventory under End— Inventory over	Over	Under	Over	Over	Y

DEBT RESTRUCTURE

Debt Impairment
1. Occurs when the probability of the amount owed will not be collected.
    a. **Debtor**
        i. Makes no entry for impairment.
        ii. Has a legal obligation to pay the debt based on the agreed upon terms.
    b. **Creditor**
        i. Determines the amount of debt that will be collectible.
        ii. The new amount is recorded at present value.
        iii. The difference between the new and old debt is recorded as an impairment.

Bad debt expense	$$$	
Note receivable impairment		$$$

Example:

1/1 creditor issued $100,000 3 year noninterest bearing note yielding 7%.

0.8163	x	100,000	=	$81,630
				Present value
Present value of $1		*Face amount*		*amount*
at 7% - 3 pds				

7%

Date	Interest	BV
1-January		81,630
31-December	5,714	87,344
31- December	6,114	93,458
31- December	6,542	100,000

At the end of the 1st year, the creditor determines the debtor can only pay $80,000.

0.8734	x	80,000	=	$69,875
				Present value
Present value of $1		*Face amount*		*amount*
at 7% for 2 periods				

7%

Date	Interest	BV
1-January		69,875
31-December	4,891	74,766
31- December	5,234	80,000

	Old debt	$87,344
−	*New debt*	(69,875)
	Impairment	**$17,469**

Bad debt expense	*$17,469*
Note receivable impairment	*17,469*

Debt Restructure
1. Occurs when the debtor is unable to pay its debt when due.
    a. A new agreement (debt restructure) is made between debtor and creditor.
    b. Or a new agreement (debt restructure) is through the court.
2. **Types of debt restructure**
    a. **Full settlement**
        i. Debt is paid in full with:
            1. Cash
            2. And/or property
                a. A gain or loss (G/L) is recognized when property is distributed (asset disposal) to the creditor for settlement of debt by the debtor.
    b. **Modification of terms**
        i. Occurs when the original terms of the agreement have been changed.
            1. A new debt is recorded
                a. At the present value (PV) of principal and interest.
                    i. Using the old interest rate.
            2. A loan impairment is recorded.
                a. And amortized over the remaining life of the debt.
                b. A G/L is recognized on the modification of terms using the effective interest rate method.
3. **Fair value (FV) method**
    a. The fair value method can be used at the onset of the debt.
        i. Debt is recorded at fair market value (FMV).
            a. Unrealized G/L is recognized as the difference between book value (BV) and FMV of the debt.
4. Financial disclosure
    a. Financial statements
        i. Balance sheet
        ii. Payable (debtor)
            1. Current
            2. Noncurrent (LT) portion
        iii. Receivable (Creditor)
            1. Current
            2. Noncurrent (LT)
        iv. Income statement
            1. Interest income (creditor)
            2. Interest expense (debtor)
    b. Notes to financial statements
        i. Debt restructure agreement should state
            1. Principle amount due
                a. paid in

      i.   Lump sum payment

      ii. Or installment payments.

          1. A schedule of payments should indicate the amount due for the first five years.

          2. A schedule of payments should indicate lump sum amount for the balance due after the first five years.

  2. Interest rate should be indicated.

  3. Due date(s) should be indicated.

Types of Debt Restructure

1. **Full Settlement—paid in full.**

Calculate Gain or loss (G/L) on Debt Settlement

Example:

Book value (BV) of debt	*$200*
Accrued interest	*8*
– Paid cash	*- 100*
– Property distributed at FMV	*—60*
G/L—Debt settlement	*$ 48*

Lender

Cash rcvd < Owed = **Loss – Debt restructure** (received less than what was owed.)

   $160   208 $ 48 Loss

Debtor

•   Cash Paid < Owed = **Gain – Debt restructure** (paid less than what was owed.)

     $160   208 $ 48 Gain

Debtor

•   Distrbuted property to the creditor as part of the agreement to settle the debt.

        FMV—Property $60

Less: NBV—Property -55

        G/L Recognized $ 5 = Gain recognized on asset disposal

Record the settlement of debt

Creditor			Debtor		
Cash received	$100		Note payable—Current	$ 18	
Property received at FMV	60		Note payable	182	
Loss—Debt restructure	48		Interest payable—Current	2	
Note receivable—Current		18	Interest payable—LT	6	
Note receivable—LT		182	Cash paid		100
Interest receivable—Current		2	Property distributed at NBV		55
Interest receivable—LT		6	Gain—asset disposal		5
			Gain—debt restructure		48

2. **Modification of Terms**

Example:

	Old	New
Principal	300	250
Accrued interest expense/income:	27	27 is forgiven
Interest rate:	9%	6%
Due date:	12/31/10	12/31/12

BOP—Beginning of period
EOP—End of period

1. **Determine book value (BV) of new debt at signing**

Principle $250 x PV at old rate (9%) .77218	=	Principle at PV $193.0450
+ Interest 15 x PV at BOP or EOP at old rate 2.5313	=	Interest at PV 37.9695
Book value (BV) of new debt at signing		$231.0145

2. **Determine loan impairment—valuation allowance at signing**

Principle - New debt	$ 250.0000
Less: BV - New debt at signing	—231.0145 ◄
Valuation allowance—Loan impairment	$ 18.9855

3. **Determine G/L on debt restructure**

	BV—Old debt	$300.0000
	Interest forgiven	27.0000
Less:	BV - New debt at signing	-231.0145
	G/L—Debt restructure	$95.9855

- Cash received < owed = **Loss**. Bad debt expense (**lender**)
  - Lender's loss is recorded as bad debt expense.
- Cash paid < owed = **Gain**. Debt restructure (**debtor**)
  - Debtor's gain is recorded as gain on debt restructure.

4. **Amortize loan impairment—valuation allowance over the life of the debt**
   - Using the effective interest rate method

BV - New-debt $231.0145 x Old interest rate 9% =	Interest expense or revenue $ 20.7913
Less: Principle—new debt 250 x New interest rate 6% =	Interest. payable or receivable -15.0000
Amortized—Valuation Allowance	**$ 5.7913**

5. **Determine book value of new debt at end of period**

Amortized—Valuation allowance	$ 5.7913
+ BV—New debt	231.0145
BV—New debt at period end	$236.8058

Lender

Record modification of terms

Bad Debt Expense	$95.99	
Note receivable		50.00
Interest receivable		27.00
Valuation allowance—Loan impairment		18.99

Record amortization of loan impairment

Interest receivable	$15.00	
Valuation allowance—Loan impairment	5.79	
Interest revenue		20.79

Debtor

Record modification of terms

Note payable	$50.00	
Interest payable	27.00	
Valuation allowance—Loan impairment	18.99	
Gain—Debt restructure		95.99

Record amortization of loan impairment

Interest expense	$20.79	
Interest payable		15.00
Valuation allowance—Loan impairment		5.79

DEPRECIATION

Depreciation Methods
*   SL—Straight line, include salvage value in calculation.
*   SYD—Sum of the year digits, include salvage value in calculation.
*   DB—Declining balance—include salvage value in calculation.
*   UOP—Units of production, include salvage value in calculation.
*   Composite (group) method, include salvage value in calculation.

Salvage value—residual value of an asset at the end of its useful life. The estimated fair value (FV) of the asset at the end of its useful life

Example:
Determine depreciation expense and accumulated depreciation in year 2.

    1/1 Copier—Office equipment
            Asset cost: $35,000
            Salvage or residual value: 5,000
            Asset life: 5 years
            Total units produced—copies: 75,000

Journal entry to record purchase

Office equipment	$35,000	
Cash or AP		$35,000

Straight Line (SL) Method $30,000 $6,000 x 2 years = **$12,000**

Asset basis:	$35,000	$\underline{\text{Depreciable basis}}$ = Depreciation expense
- Salvage value:	- 5,000	Useful life – 5 years
Depreciable basis:	$30,000	

Asset basis	$35,000 1/1/17	Depreciation expense $ 6,000	Income statement (I/S)
- Accumulated depreciation—**12,000** (yr. 2)		Accumulated depreciation 6,000	Balance sheet (BS)
Net book value (NBV)	$23,000 12/31/18		

Sum of the Year Digits (SYD) Method

Asset basis:	$35,000		Year	Method
- Salvage value:	- 5,000		1	5 ⎫
Depreciable basis:	$30,000		2	4 ⎬ x 30,000 = **$18,000** Deprec. exp. for 2 years
			3	3 15 Depreciable basis = $30,000
Asset basis	$35,000	1/1/17	4	2
- Accumulated Depreciation - **18,000**			5	1 5 x 30 = $10,000 Year 1
Net Book Value (NBV)	$17,000	12/31/18	15	15

76

I/S Depreciation expense $10 $8 for year 1and2 $\underline{4}$ x 30 = $8,000 Year 2

BS   Accumulated depreciation 10 8   15

Double Declining Balance (DDB) Method

Asset basis:	$35,000	$30,000 x .40 = $12,000 Depreciation expense Year 1
- Salvage value:	- 5,000	- 12,000
Depreciable basis:	$30,000	$18,000 x .40 = $7,200 Depreciation expense Year 2

$19,200 is total depreciation for 2 years

Asset basis	$35,000 1/1/17	
- Accumulation Depreciation	- **19,200**	$\underline{1}$ = .20 x 2 = .40 Double declining
Net book value (NBV)	$15,800 12/31/18	5 years

I/S Depreciation expense	$12	$7.2
BS Accumulated depreciation	12	7.2

Units of Production (UOP) Method

		$30,000	$.40
Asset basis:	$35,000	Depreciable basis	= Cost per unit
- Salvage value:	- 5,000	Total units produced	
Depreciable basis	$30,000	75,000	

Units produced

Asset basis	$35,000 1/1/17	Year 1 9,000 x .40 = $ 3,600
- Accumulated depreciation	- 8,400	Year 2 12,000 x .40 = 4,800
Net book value (NBV)	$26,600 12/31/18	Total depreciation $8,400

Year	1	2
I/S Depreciation expense	$3,600	$4,800
BS Accumulated depreciation	3,600	4,800

Composite (Group) Method

Example: Fleet of (4) limo cars (4) at $35,000 each
(4) Delivery Trucks at $35,000 each
Salvage value—cars and trucks: (2) at $6,000 and (2) at $4,000

Asset basis	$140,000 = 8 vehicles at $35,000 each
- Salvage value	- 20,000 = 2 x $6,000 + 2 x $4,000
Depreciable basis	$ 120,000

Asset basis	$140,000	
- Accumulated depreciation	- 24,000	
Net book value (NBV)	$ 116,000	

I/S Depreciation expense	$24,000	
BS Accumulated depreciation		$24,000

$120,000 $24,000

Sum—Depreciable basis   = Sum - Depreciation expense

Average useful life 5 years

Composite (Group) Method

1. Group of similar assets or category of assets (fleet of limo cars or delivery trucks)
2. Determine sum of cost: sum all asset cost in the group or category
3. Determine sum of depreciable basis: sum the depreciable basis of all assets in the group or category
4. Determine sum of residual value: sum the salvage or residual value of all assets in the group or category.
5. Determine sum of depreciation expense: sum the depreciation expense of all assets in the group or category.

Composite (Group) Method

- Depreciation expense of $24,000 will be deducted for the remaining useful life (5 years) of the assets until additions or disposals occur.
- Additions to the group result in a new depreciation rate and Average Useful Life calculation.
- Disposals a sale or discard of an asset from the group results in a new depreciation rate and the Average Useful Life is recalculated.
  - No gain or loss is recognized on asset disposal.
    - The gain or loss is applied against accumulated depreciation.

Example:

Sold a vehicle for $25,000.

Cash	$25,000	
Accumulated Depreciation	10,000	is a plug that includes the gain or loss recognized.
Cost	$35,000	

Overview

1/1	**Cost**	**$35**	**$35**	**$35**	**$35**
	Year	**SL**	**SYD**	**DDB**	**UOP**
	1	$ 6	$10	$12.0	$ 3.6
	2	6	8	7.2	4.8
Accum. depreciation		$ 12	$18	$19.2	$8.4
12/31	**NBV**	$23	$17	$15.8	$26.6

Gain on Disposal

1/1 Proceeds	$25	$25	$25.0	
- NBV	- 23	- 17	- 15.8	
1/1 Gain disposal	2	8	9.2	

Loss on Disposal

1/1	Proceeds	$12	$12	$12.0	$ 12.0
	- NBV	- 23	- 17	- 15.8	- 26.6
1/1	Loss disposal	- 11	- 5	- 3.8	- 14.6

Asset Disposal

Sale:

Gain—Sale of SYD			Loss—Sale of SYD		
Cash	$25		Cash	$ 12	
Accumulated depreciation	18		Accumulated depreciation	18	
Asset		35	Loss—Disposal		5
Gain—disposal		8	Asset		35

Retirement of Asset:

Loss—Asset Retirement of SL

Accumulated depreciation	$12	
Loss—disposal	23	
Asset		35

Relationship Overview

Method	Accumulated Depreciation	Net Income	New Book Value	Gain	Loss	Salvage Value
DDB	Highest $19.2	Lowest due to highest depreciation	Lowest $15.8	Highest $9.2	Lowest $- 3.8	Y
SYD	Mid $18	Mid	Mid $17	Mid $8	Mid $ - 5	Y
SL	Lowest $12	Highest due to lowest depreciation	Highest $23	Lowest $2	Highest $ -11	Y
UOP	Varies depending upon the units produced.					Y

79

DERIVATIVE INSTRUMENTS

Financial Instrument (FI)
1. Include
   a. Cash
   b. Stocks
   c. Evidence of ownership interest in an entity (e.g.; corporation, partnership, LLC); partial list:
      i. Common stock
      ii. Preferred stock
      iii. Stock options
   d. Bonds
   e. Payables
   f. Receivables
   g. Foreign currency (FC) forward contracts
   h. Future contracts
   i. Financial swaps
2. Excludes—LIPP
   a. **L**eases
   b. **I**nsurance contracts
   c. **P**ension plans
   d. **P**ostretirement benefit plans
3. Disclosure
   a. Financial statements
      i. Balance sheet
         1. As an asset or liability at fair value
      ii. Income statement
         1. Changes in FV are recorded as unrealized gainor loss as part of income from continuing operations
4. Notes to Financial statement
   a. Report the class or category of the financial instrument.
   b. Assumption used to estimate fair value.
   c. Credit risk
   d. Cross reference when used in other areas of the financial statements.

Derivative Instruments (DI)
1. Financial instruments (FI) that derive their value from factors independent of the financial instrument.
   a. Contain
      i. An underlying
         1. Represents the Unit cost of the derivative
            a. Example:
               i. Stock price
               ii. Interest rate
               iii. Mortgage rate
               iv. Currency rate
               v. Commodity price
               vi. Credit rate
               vii. Insurance index

        viii. Temperature
- ii. A notional amount
  1. Represents the quantity associated with the derivative.
     - a. Example:
       - i. Shares
       - ii. Principal
       - iii. Face value
       - iv. Points
  - b. Disclosure
    - i. Financial statement
      - a. As an asset or liability at fair value
    2. Income statement changes in fair value are recorded as unrealized gainor loss as part of income from continuing operations.
       - a. Changes in fair value
  - c. Notes to the financial statements
    - i. Reported as required

Derivative Instruments (DI)

1. Include
   - a. Stock call (buyback) options
   - b. Stock put (issue) options
   - c. Future contracts
   - d. Forward contracts
   - e. Credit index contracts
   - f. Interest rate swaps
   - g. Currency swaps
   - h. Interest rate caps
2. Exclude
   - a. Equity securities
   - b. Debt securities
   - c. Leases
   - d. Variable annuity contracts
   - e. Adjustable rate loans
   - f. Mortgage-backed securities
   - g. Employee stock options
   - h. Royalty agreements
   - i. Guaranteed investment contracts

Call (buyback) Option	Unit Cost	Purchase amount
In the money	Underlying	> Strike or exercise price
At the money	Underlying	= Strike or exercise price
Out the money	Underlying	< Strike or exercise price

Put (issue) Option	Unit Cost	Issue price
In the money	Underlying	< Strike or exercise price
At the money	Underlying	= Strike or exercise price
Out the money	Underlying	> Strike or exercise price

Derivative Instruments contain

- Underlying—the variable affecting the value of the derivative instrument.
  - Derives its value from a factor outside or separate from the instrument itself; for example, market rate.
- Notational amount—referred to in terms of units, quantity, etc.
- No initial net investment or investment less than the required contract is required.
- Terms for settlement are the same as any normal investment.

Derivative Instrument (DI)

- Derives its value from the underlying.
- Is categorized as a financial instrument.
- Classified as an Asset or Liability
- Recorded at fair value (FV).
- Unrealized Gains or losses resulting from changes in fair value are recorded in
  - Other comprehensive income.
  - Income from continuing operations
- Is a hybrid instrument
- Contains an embedded derivative instrument (EDI) and a host.
  - Separating the EDI from the host is called bifurcation.
    - Bifurcation is appropriate for valuating and recording the hybrid instrument.
      - The host and EDI are independent nonrelated components.
      - Host is recorded at book value.
      - EDI is recorded at fair value.
      - EDI is a DI.
  - Example—hybrid instrument
    - Bond payable (host)—interest rate—attached to S&P 500 (EDI).
    - Equity instruments—with a call or put option.
    - Loans (host) based on short term treasury bills or prime rate (EDI).
    - Convertible debt (debt to equity security)

Types of Derivatives

- **Swap agreement**—agreement used to reduce interest rate risk.
- **Forward contract**—a transaction meant to minimize changes in currency rates at a specific date in the future.
- **Future contract**—a contract meant to reduce the risk of loss associated with an asset purchase in the future.
- **Option**—gives the buyer the right to buy or sell a financial instrument at a specific price on a specific date.
  - The seller has the obligation to satisfy the transaction if the buyer exercises the option; for example, stock options.

Asset or Liability

- **Hedged** - is meant to protect parties from adverse changes in the underlying.
  - Hedging protects against changes in Fair Value (FV) or Cash flow (CF).
    - The risk management of hedging
      - Must be **supported by sufficient documentation** regarding the financial instrument.
      - The hedging transaction must be **highly effective** throughout the life of instrument.
- **Non-hedged**—is a normal investment purchase.
  - The hedging component is not part of the purchase.

Hedging
- Designed to minimizing changes in value of a specific item.
- Requires supporting documentation.
- Must be highly effective over the life of the hedging activity.
- Hedging Instrument
  - Unrecognized firm commitment
  - Is a binding agreement to purchase
  - Specific terms and conditions.
  - Performance clause may be included to ensure performance
- Hedging activity
  - Available for sale (AFS) security
  - Foreign currency (FC) forecast transaction
  - Net investment in foreign operations (Ops)
- Hedging transaction - purpose is to minimize changes in:
  - FV—fair value
  - FC—foreign currency
  - CF—cash flow

Type of Hedge
1. **Fair value (FV)**
   a. Pertains to
      i. Assets
      ii. Liabilities
      iii. Firm commitments
   b. Reports changes in
      i. Fair value of asset
      ii. Fair value of liability
      iii. Fair value—unrecognized firm commitment
   c. Reports changes in fair value
      i. In the Income statement as part of income from continuing operations
2. **Cash Flow (CF)**
   a. reports changes in cash flow
      i. pertaining to
         1. Assets
         2. Liabilities
         3. Forecasted transactions.
   b. Effective portion is reported in other comprehensive income (OCI).
      i. The effective portion—indicates the effectiveness in offsetting changes in fair value that affect the cash flow of the instrument.
         1. The hedge offsets changes in cash flow.
      ii. Ineffective portion is reported in the income statement as part of income from continuing operations.
3. **Foreign Currency - Fair Value**
   a. Pertains to
      i. Unrecognized firm commitments
      ii. Available-for-sale securities
      iii. Forecasted transactions
      iv. Net investments in foreign operations
   b. Reports changes in fair value as part of income from continuing operations
   c. Gain or loss of Hedging is reported as part of income from continuing operations.

4. **Foreign Currency - Cash flow**
   a. pertains to
      i. Unrecognized firm commitments
      ii. Available-for-sale securities
      iii. Forecasted transactions
      iv. Net investments in foreign operations
   b. Reports changes in cash flow resulting from foreign currency fluctuations
      i. Effective portion is reported in other comprehensive income (OCI).
      ii. Ineffective portion is reported in the income statement as part of income from continuing operations.
5. **Investment in Foreign Operations**
   c. Reports changes in the foreign currency fluctuation of the investment in OCI.

Example of Hedging
- A company enters into a firm commitment agreement with a foreign supplier to purchase equipment.
   - The purchase price is in foreign currency.
   - Delivery and payment are in the future.
   - The transaction may be classified as a hedge to protect against changes in foreign currency from date of agreement to date of payment.
   - The period between the commitment date and delivery date are a hedge against unrecognized firm commitment (fair value recognition).
   - The period between the delivery date and payment date are a hedge against recognized liability (cash flow recognition).

Hedge Overview

Transaction	Instrument	G/L Recognition—Hedging
FV Hedge	• Assets or liabilities	Income from continuing operations
	• Unrecognized firm commitments	
FC Hedge	• Unrecognized from commitment	
	• AFS securities	Income from continuing operations
	• FC forecast transaction	
	• Net investment—foreign ops other comprehensive income (OCI)	
	• Hedge accounting is not applicable.	
	• SFAS 52 applies.	
CF Hedge	• Asset and liabilities	OCI—effective portion (successful hedge transaction)
	• FC forecast transaction	Inc. continuing operations, ineffective portion (unsuccessful hedge transaction)

Embedded Derivative Instrument (EDI)
- Hybrid instrument
   - Not recorded at fair value.
   - Financial instrument with an embedded derivative instrument.
      - Bifurcation—the process of separating the components of the instrument.

- Host—is the financial instrument
- Valued using financial instrument rules.
- Derivative instrument—is the derivative
  - Valued using derivative rules
  - Reported as part of
    - Other comprehensive income
    - Or income from continuing operations as part of earnings.
  - May elect *not* to bifurcate the hybrid instrument on an instrument-by-instrument basis.
  - The instrument is valued at fair value.
  - Reports changes in fair value as part of income from continuing operations

Examples:
Bond—interest rate is based on Sandards & Poor's 500.
Stock with a call option—allows the issuing company to buy back the stock.
Stock with a put option—requires the issuing company to buy back the stock at the purchaser's request.
Loan—**penalty** for early payoff is based on T-bill rates.

Description	Host	Derivative instrument
Stock Price	Stock	Market price
Mortgage	Mortgage	Interest rate
Commodity	Commodity	Price
Currency	Denomination	Value

DEVELOPMENTAL STAGE ENTERPRISE

Developmental Stage Enterprise
- FASB statement #7 (ASC Topic 915—Developmental Stage Enterprises)
- A company/entity in the developmental stages.
- The start of a new business that has not begun operations or has not generated sufficient revenue in its initial stages of operation.
- This usually occurs during the early years of a new business startup.

Startup Cost
- ASC 720—Startup cost (AICPA Statement of Position 98-5)
- Expense as incurred.
- Cost associated with opening a new facility, new product launch, business startup, etc.

Organization Cost
- ASC 720—Startup cost (AICPA Statement of Position 98-5)
- Expense as incurred.
- Cost associated with forming a business.
    - For example: legal fees, filing fees to incorporate or form a business, etc.

DIVIDENDS

Dividends
- Require board of directors (BOD) approval.
  - Dividend declared—a formal authorization to distribute earnings is required by the BOD
  - Earnings are decreased when dividends are declared
  - Earnings are distributed to shareholders in the form of a dividend against earnings
- Types of dividends
  - Cash
  - Liquidating
  - Scrip
  - Property
  - Stock
- Dividend transaction
  - Declared—authorization to distribute assets or equity.
    - Retained earnings is decreased and a liability is recorded.
  - Date of record—stockholders on record at the date of declaration.
    - Record—a list of who should receive the dividends.
  - Date of payment—the date dividends are to be paid.
    - The liability is settled (paid).

Cash Dividend

Cash is distributed.

Example: *Board of Directors (BOD) declared a $200 cash dividend. Payable in 30 days.*

Declared	*Record*	*Payment*
RE $200	*No entry required*	*Dividend payable $200*
Div. Payable 200		*Cash 200*

When declared, *stockholders equity (retained earnings—RE) decreased by $200.*
When paid, *cash decreased by $200.*

Recipient:
*Received $200 of **taxable dividend income**.*   *Cash $200*
                                                          Dividend Income 200

Liquidating Dividend
- Has sufficient cash or assets to make the payment.
- But insufficient Current or Accumulated earnings to cover the distribution.
  - Retained earnings (RE) is decreased.
- Resulting in a return of capital (liquidating dividend).
  - Additional paid in capital (APIC) is reduced.
- Stockholders Equity is decreased.
- Cash Distribution > Accumulated Earnings = Liquidating Dividend

	(Dividend)	• Current	(APIC)
		• Accumulated	(Return of Capital)

Example: *BOD declared a $200 cash dividend. Payable in 30 days.*

Declared	Record	Payment
RE 150	No Entry required	Dividend payable 200
APIC 50		Cash 200
Dividend payable 200		

Recipient

Received $200 of **taxable dividend income**.	Cash	200
	Dividend Income	**200**

Scrip Dividend
- An IOU issued to shareholders of record.
- Unlike a liquidating dividend which has sufficient cash but insufficient earnings.
- A scrip dividend:
    - Has insufficient cash to make the payment.
    - Has sufficient earnings to make the distribution.
    - A promissory note payable with interest is issued to shareholders of record.

Example: *BOD declared a $200 cash dividend. Payable in 6 months at 7% interest.*

Declared	Record	Payment
RE $200	No Entry required	Scrip dividend payable $200
Scrip dividend payable 200		Cash 200
Interest expense $14		Interest payable $14
Interest payable 14		Cash 14

Interest is accrued each month for 6 months.

Recipient *received $200 of* **taxable dividend income with interest**.	Cash $214	
	Interest income	14
	Scrip dividend payable	200

Property Dividend
- A distribution of property instead of cash to shareholders.
- The property is distributed at fair market value.
- A property gain or loss is recognized when declared.
- Examples of property distributed:

- Merchandise such as inventory.
- Real estate (land, buildings)
- Investments (marketable securities)

Example: *BOD declared a property dividend of marketable securities with a book value of $200. The fair market value of the securities at date of declaration is $220.*

Declared	*Record*	*Payment*

Retained earnings $200.   No entry required.   Property dividend distributable $220

Property dividend distributable   200   Marketable securities   220

Marketable Securities $20

*   Gain—Marketable securities   20*

Recipient records receipt of the property:

Receives $220 in marketable securities as **taxable dividend income**.

                                    Marketable Securities $220

                                            APIC—Property dividend. 220

Stock Dividend

- An equity distribution in the form of a stock issue.
  - There is no change in stockholders' equity as a result of the distribution.
  - No cash is distributed.
  - Common (CS) or preferred (PS) stock is issued.
  - **Common stock dividend**
    - Generally nontaxable.
    - The dividend basis is determined based on the percent ownership in the corporation.

	% Ownership	**Dividend Basis**
Large Distribution:	≥ 20—25%	Par Value or Stated
Small Distribution:	< 20—25 %	FMV

  - **Preferred Stock** (PS) **Dividend**
    - Usually taxable (some exceptions may apply).
    - May be participating, nonparticipating, cumulative, noncumulative, callable, convertible, etc.
    - Cumulative PS
      - Dividend in arrears—legal obligation to pay before CS shareholders.
        - Financial disclosure is required.
          - Paid, but not declared.
            - No financial accrual is made.
            - Notes— financial statement disclosure.
            - Or, parenthetical financial disclosure.
          - Declared, but not paid.
            - Financial accrual is made.
            - Notes— financial statement disclosure.

- Noncumulative PS
    - Dividend in arrears— no legal obligation to pay before CS shareholders.
    - No financial reporting is required.

Stock Dividend - Small Distribution is recorded at fair market value.
Issuer - journal entry to record stock dividend.
- < 20—25%
- Record at Fair Market Value (FMV).
  Declared
  > Retained Earnings FMV
  > Stock dividend distributable Par value
  > Additional Paid In Capital (APIC) Difference
  Record
  > No entry required.
  Payment
  > Stock dividend distributable   Par value
  >   Common Stock   Par value

Recipient - records receipt of stock dividend.

> Investment—corporate stock   FMV
>   APIC—Stock dividend   FMV

Stock Dividend - Large Distribution is recorded at par value.
- **Issuer** - journal entry to record stock dividend.
- > 20—25%
    - Record at Par Value.

Declared	**Record**	**Payment**
Retained Earnings Par value	No entry required.	Stock dividend distributable Par value
Stock dividend distributable Par value		Common Stock Par value

Recipient - records receipt of stock dividend.   Investment—corporate stock Par value
                                                           APIC—Stock dividend Par value

Earnings per Share

Quick glance of how the different types of stock are used in the calculation of basic earnings per share (BEPS) and diluted earnings per share (DEPS)

Type of Stock	BEPS	DEPS
Treasury stock	Yes Shares **acquired** are prorated from acquire date. Shares **issued** are prorated from issue or reissue date.	Yes Shares **acquired** are prorated from acquire date. Shares **issued** are prorated from issue or reissue date.
Common stock	Yes Shares **acquired** are prorated from acquire date. Shares **issued** are prorated from issue or reissue date.	Yes Shares **acquired** are prorated from acquire date. Shares **issued** are prorated from issue or reissue date.
Preferred stock	No	No
Stock splits	Yes Declared during the year—use full year in calculation.	Yes Declared during the year—use full year in calculation.
Reverse stock split	Yes Declared during the year—use full year in calculation.	Yes Declared during the year—use full year in calculation.
Stock options	No or Yes Unexercised—no action required. Exercised—from date of exercise.	Yes Unexercised—use full year in calculation. And, determine diluted shares. Exercised—from date of exercise.
Warrants	No or Yes Unexercised—no action required. Exercised—from date of exercise.	Yes Unexercised—use full yr. in calculation. Exercised—from date of exercise.

Convertible preferred stock	No or Yes Not converted—no action required. Converted—from date of exercise.	Yes Not converted—use full yr. in calculation. Converted—from date of exercise.

Type of Stock	BEPS	DEPS
Preferred stock dividend	Used in numerator. Not declared—assume declared. Declared—use amount declared. Paid, Not declared—use calculated PS dividend not paid amount. Use paid amount if calculated PS dividend is unknown. Cumulative PS dividend calculate whether declared or not. PS dividends for the current year are used. Dividends in arrears are included in the year in which they pertain. Noncumulative PS dividends calculate using declared only.	Used in numerator. Not declared—assume declared. Declared—use amount declared. Paid, not declared—use calculated PS dividend not paid amount. Use paid amount if calculated PS dividend is unknown. Cumulative PS dividend—calculate whether or not declared. PS dividends for the current year are used. Dividends in arrears are not included in current year EPS calculation. Noncumulative PS dividends— calculate using declared only.
Contingent shares	No or Yes Unexercised—no action required. Exercised—from date of exercise.	Yes Unexercised—use full year in calculation. Exercised—from date of exercise.
Common stock dividend	Yes Declared during the year—use full year in calculation.	Yes Declared during the year—use full year in calculation.
Stock rights	No or Yes Unexercised—no action required. Exercised—from date of exercise.	Yes Unexercised—use full year in calculation. Exercised—from date of exercise.

Convertible bonds	No	Yes
	Not converted—numerator includes bond net of tax for the full period. Denominator no shares are assumed converted. Converted—numerator includes bonds prorated net of tax for the period not converted. Denominator no shares are assumed converted. Only the converted shares are used in the calculation	Not converted—Numerator includes Bond net of tax for the full period. Denominator includes bonds assumed converted for the full year. Converted "as if" 1/1 of the current year. Converted—numerator includes bonds pro-rated net of tax for the period not converted. Denominator includes the shares pro-rated (from date of conversion to end of period) for the period converted. Plus, nonconverted shares prorated for the period not converted.

Earnings per Share (EPS)

Required for publically traded companies.

	EPS	
Income from continuing operations—net of tax	$. $ $	Reporting required.
Discontinued operations—net of tax	$. $ $	Reporting is not required.
Extraordinary item—Net of tax	$. $ $	
Net income (NI)	$. $ $	Reporting required.

Determine the Number of Outstanding Shares

		O/s	Issued	Div.	T.S.
1/1 Outstanding shares 100	1/1 O/s	100	100		
4/1 20 Shares issued	4/1 Issued	20	20		
		120			
6/1 Dividend declared 10%	6/1 10% Dividend	12		12	
		132			
10/1 10 Shares acquired	10/1 Acquired	-10			-10
		122			
11/1 Declared 2:1 stock split	11/1 2:1 Split	122	120	12	-10
		244	**240**	**24**	**-20**

Determine the Weighted Average of Shares

Option # 1—Use Transactional Method | **Option # 2**—Use Totals Method

Option # 1:

January to December

1/1 - O/S $100 \times 2 \times \dfrac{12}{12} = \mathbf{200}$

Split Apr to Dec

4/1 - Issue $\underline{20} \times 2 \times 9/12 = \mathbf{30}$
Total: 120

Split January to December

6/1—10 % Div. $12 \times 2 \times \dfrac{12}{12} = \mathbf{24}$
Total: 132

Split October to December

10/1—Acquired $\underline{-10} \times 2 \times \dfrac{3}{12} = \mathbf{-5}$
Total: 122   249

Option # 2:

January to May

January - May O/S - $120 \times 2 \times \dfrac{5}{12} = \mathbf{100}$
1 to 31   Split

June to Sept

June—Sept O/S - $132 \times 2 \times \dfrac{4}{12} = \mathbf{88}$
                              Split

October to December

October to December O/S - $\underline{122} \times 2 \times \dfrac{3}{12} = \underline{\mathbf{61}}$
                                     Split   **249**

11/1 Stock split is reflected in the weighted average as 2x.

Earnings per Share (EPS)

Method 1—Using Stocks

DEPS = $\dfrac{\text{Net income (NI) less PS dividend}}{\text{Weighted average of outstanding shares + dilutive shares}}$

BEPS = $\dfrac{\text{Net income (NI) less PS dividend.}}{\text{Weighted average of outstanding shares}}$

Method 2—Using Stocks and Bonds

DEPS = $\dfrac{\text{Net income (NI) + Bond interest—Net of tax}}{\text{Weighted average of outstanding shares + dilutive Share}}$

BEPS = $\dfrac{\text{Net Income (NI) + Bond interest—Net of tax}}{\text{Weighted average of outstanding shares}}$

Under both methods
- Weighted average outstanding shares usually represents common stock shares unless otherwise stated.
- Dilutive test
  - Stock option (exercise) price < market price
    - Determine the amount of dilutive shares.
  - The dilutive shares are common stock and/or common stock equivalents.

- Antidilutive EPS.
  - The exercise price > market value.

Examples of Dilutive Shares
- Stock splits
- Stock options
- Stock warrants
- Convertible bonds
- Convertible preferred stock
- Contingent shares

Stock Split
- Stock split has not occurred—assume full year, as if 1/1 of current year.
- Stock split has occurred—prorate from date of split to period end date.

Stock Options
- Exercised—prorate from date of exercise to period end date.
- Unexercised
  - If dilutive
    - Option price < market price
    - Assume exercised for the full year, as if 1/1 of current year.

Unexercised stock option shares times exercise price = **Average stock option shares**
Average market price of stock option

     Unexercised stock option shares (shares assumed issued)
Less: **Average stock option shares** (shares assumed repurchased)
     Dilutive stock option shares

- If antidilutive
  - Option price > market price
  - Shares are not applicable or included in the calculation of DEPS.

Example:
   Dilutive: Option price < Market price
        $20   < $25   Unexercised stock options 20,000 shares

20,000 shares times $20 option price = $400,000 = Assumed repurchased shares 16,000
                        $25 Market price

Unexercised shares	*20,000*
- Assumed repurchased	*- 16,000*
Dilutive shares	***4,000***

Example:
   Antidilutive: *Option price > Market price*
        $20   > $15 Unexercised stock options 20,000 shares

20,000 shares times $20 option price = $400,000 = Assumed repurchased shares 26,667
                        $15 Market price

Unexercised shares	*20,000*
– Assumed repurchased	*– 26,667*
Antidilutive shares	***6,667***

Stock warrants
- Exercised—prorate from date of exercise.
- Unexercised—assume full year, as if 1/1 of current year.

Convertibles
- Conversion has not taken place—assume converted for full year, as if 1/1 of current year.
- Converted shares—prorate from date of conversion.

Contingent shares
- Contingency met—prorate from the date the contingency occurred.
- Contingency not met—assume full year, as if 1/1 of current year.

Example—Preferred stock:
1/1 10,000 shares PS $10 par at 5%. Net income for the period is $450,000. 285,000 CS shares were outstanding at 1/1. No other shares were issued.

$1.5614 $450,000 less $5,000

$$DEPS = \frac{\underline{Net\ Income\ less\ Preferred\ stock\ dividend}}{Weighted\ average\ of\ outstanding\ shares + Dilutive\ shares}$$

285,000 shares   + 0 dilutive shares

- *In general,*
  - *PS dividends are deducted from net income (NI) declared or not.*
    - *PS dividends paid but not declared are deducted.*
  - *PS dividend = PS shares x Par value x Dividend %*
  - ***$5,000***   *=   10,000   x $10   x 5%*

Example—Convertible preferred stock, not converted:
1/1 10,000 shares PS $10 par 5% convertible into 20,000 Shares C.S $5 par. Net income for the period is $450,000. 285,000 CS shares were outstanding at 1/1. No other shares were issued.

$1.4754 $450,000 less PS Div. not applicable

$$DEPS = \frac{\underline{Net\ Income\ less\ Preferred\ stock\ dividend}}{Weighted\ average\ of\ outstanding\ shares + Dilutive\ shares}$$

285,000 shares   + 20,000 dilutive shares

- *Convertible PS that has not yet been converted.*
- *PS dividend is not included in the calculation.*
- *Nonconverted shares are assumed converted for the full year.*

$1.5789 = $450,000 less not applicable

$$BEPS = \frac{\underline{Net\ Income\ less\ Preferred\ stock\ dividend}}{Weighted\ average\ of\ outstanding\ shares} = 285,000\ shares$$

Example—Convertible preferred stock, converted:
1/1 10,000 PS shares, $10 par 5% are converted April 1 into 20,000 CS shares $5 par. Net income for the period is $450,000. 285,000 CS shares were outstanding at 1/1. No other shares were issued.

PS is converted April 1
- *PS dividend calculation is prorated **to** date of conversion.*

- Converted shares are prorated from date of conversion

$$10{,}000 \text{ PS shares} \times \$10 \text{ PS par} \times 5\% \text{ PS dividend} \times \frac{3}{12} = \$1{,}250 \text{ PS dividend}$$

January– March (3 months) represents the nonconverted period.

$$20{,}000 \text{ shares CS} \times \frac{9}{12} = 15{,}000 \text{ CS shares}$$

April– December (9 months) represents the period the PS shares were converted into CS shares.

$1.4958 \qquad \$450,000 \text{ less } \$1,250$

DEPS = <u>Net Income less Preferred stock dividend</u>

Weighted average of outstanding shares + Dilutive shares

285,000 shares   + 15,000 shares

$1.5746 = \$450,000 \text{ less } \$1,250$

BEPS = <u>Net Income less Preferred stock dividend</u>

Weighted average of outstanding shares = 285,000 shares

Example—ordinary bond:

1/1 (30) $1,000 Bonds at 7%. Tax rate 28%. Net income for the period is $450,000. 285,000 CS shares were outstanding at 1/1. No other shares were issued.

30 Bonds x $1,000 per bond x 7% Bond interest rate = $2,100 x 28% = $588

Bond interest Amount x Tax rate = Tax $$

Bond Interest:	$2,100
Less: <u>Tax</u>	- <u>588</u>
Bond interest—Net of tax	**$1,512**

$1.5784 \quad \$450,000 + \mathbf{\$1,512}$

DEPS = <u>Net Income + Bond interest—Net of tax</u>

Weighted average of outstanding shares + Dilutive shares

285,000 shares   + 0 dilutive shares

$1.5784 \quad \$450,000 + \mathbf{\$1,512}$

BEPS = <u>Net Income + Bond interest—Net of tax</u>

Weighted average of outstanding shares = 285,000 shares

Example—Convertible bond not converted under the book value method:

- Bond interest— net of tax is not applicable.
  - Assumed bonds are converted.
- Nonconverted shares—assume converted for the full year

Example:

1/1 (30) $1,000 bonds at 6% are convertible into 300 shares of $5 par CS per bond. Net income for the period is $450,000. 285,000 CS shares were outstanding at 1/1. No other shares were issued.

$1.5306 = $450,000 + not applicable

$$DEPS = \frac{Net\ Income + Bond\ interest—Net\ of\ tax}{Weighted\ average\ of\ outstanding\ shares + Dilutive\ shares}$$

285,000 shares   **+ 9,000 dilutive shares**

Nonconverted shares
30 Bonds x 300 shares CS = **9,000 Shares** CS

Example—Convertible bonds converted under the book value method:

- Bond interest—net of tax is prorated during the period to date of conversion.
- Converted shares— prorated from date of conversion to end of period.

1/1 (30) $1,000 Bonds at 6% are converted April 1 into 300 shares of CS per bond. Tax rate is 28%. Net income for the period is $450,000. At 1/1, 285,000 CS shares were outstanding. No other shares were issued.

30 Bonds x $1,000 per bond x 6% Bond interest rate x $\frac{3}{12}$ = $450 x 28% = $126
Bond interest Amount x Tax rate = Tax $$

Bond interest**:**	$450
Less: Tax	- 126
Bond interest—Net of tax	$ 324

$1.544 $450,000 less not applicable+ 324

$$DEPS = \frac{Net\ Income\ less\ PS\ Dividends + Bond\ interest—Net\ of\ tax}{Weighted\ average\ of\ outstanding\ shares + Dilutive\ shares\ CS}$$

285,000 shares   **+ 6,750 shares**

Converted Shares
      30 Bonds x 300 Shares CS = 9,000 CS x 9/12 = **6,750** C.S **shares** pro-rated
April to December (9 months) represents the nonconverted period.

Example—Complex example:

Net income for the period was $300,000.

1/1 Common stock (CS) outstanding 200,000 shares.

4/1 Common stock issued 40,000 shares.

Convertible bond (50) at $1,000 each at 12% interest. Each bond converts into 1,000 CS shares. Tax rate 35%.

Convertible Preferred stock (PS) 1,000 shares at $100 par value at 10%. The 1,000 PS shares convert into 2,000 CS shares.

Stock options, 1,000 CS shares at $15 exercise price. And, 1,000 CS shares at $25 exercise price. Average common stock market value is $20.

Solution

Net income *for the period was* **$300,000**.

1/1 CS outstanding 200,000 shares. = **200,000 CS shares outstanding.**

4/1 CS issued 40,000 shares = 40,000 x 9/12 = **30,000 CS shares outstanding.**

April to December (9 months) represents the nonconverted period.

Convertible bond (50) at $1,000 each at 12% Interest. Each bond converts into 1,000 CS shares. Tax rate 35%.

(50) Bonds x 1,000 CS shares = **50,000 CS shares assumed converted**.

(50) Bonds x $1,000 each x 12% = $6,000 x (1 - 35% = 65%) **= $3,900 Bond interest net of tax.**

Convertible PS 1,000 shares at $100 par value at 10%. The 1,000 PS shares convert into 2,000 CS shares.

1,000 PS shares convert into 2,000 CS shares = **2,000 CS shares assumed converted.**

Stock options, 1,000 CS shares at $15 exercise price. And, 1,000 CS shares at $25 exercise price. Average common stock market value is $20.

1,000 CS shares at exercise price $15 < Market value $20 is Dilutive.

1,000 CS shares x $15 = $15,000 = 750 Assumed exercised
                    $20 Market value

> *1,000 CS shares Unexercised*
> *- 750 Assumed exercised*
> **250 Dilutive shares**

1,000 CS shares at exercise price $25 > Market value $20 is antidilutive, and is not considered in the equation.

$1.0767 = $300,000 less ($10k less $10k assumed converted) + $3,900 Bond interest net of tax
DEPS = Net Income less PS Dividends + Bond interest—Net of tax
        Weighted average of outstanding shares + Dilutive shares CS
            200,000 shares at 1/1 + 30,000 shares at 4/1 + 50,000 CS shares assumed converted + 2,000 CS shares assumed converted + 250 Stock option

$1.2609 = $300,000 less $10,000 + Not applicable
BEPS = Net Income less PS Dividends + Bond interest—Net of tax
        Weighted average of outstanding shares
            200,000 shares at 1/1 + 30,000 shares at 4/1

FINANCIAL RATIOS

Ratios

- Dividends per share (DPS) = $\dfrac{\text{Total dividend paid}}{\text{Total outstanding shares adjusted for treasury stock (stock buyback)}}$

    Dividends per share is a ratio of dividends to outstanding shares.

- Dividend payout = $\dfrac{\text{Dividends per share}}{\text{Earnings per share}}$ or $\dfrac{\text{Dividends}}{\text{Net income}}$

Dividend payout ratio is an indication of how much is returned to shareholders in the form of dividends.

- Rate of return on equity = $\dfrac{\text{Net income}}{\text{Stockholders' equity}}$

The rate of return on equity relates to common stock. Net Income (NI) is adjusted for PS dividends and CS dividends. And, stockholders' equity (SHE) is adjusted for preferred stock. O/s is the abbreviation for outstanding shares.

- Debt to equity = $\dfrac{\text{Total debt}}{\text{Stockholders' equity}}$

- Basic earnings per share (BEPS) = $\dfrac{\text{NI less PS dividend}}{\text{Weighted average of outstanding shares}}$

- Diluted earnings per share (DEPS) = $\dfrac{\text{NI less PS dividend}}{\text{Weighted average of outstanding shares + Diluted shares}}$

- DEPS = $\dfrac{\text{NI + Bond interest—Net of tax}}{\text{Weighted average + Convertible shares}}$

Financial Ratios

Deb-to-equity ratio = $\dfrac{\text{Total liabilities}}{\text{Stockholders' equity}}$

- Debt-to-equity ratio is an indicator of debt to equity.
- The lower the ratio, the better.
- A low ratio indicates there is less debt to capital.

Financial Ratios

Working capital

       Current assets
       - <u>Current liabilities</u>
       Working capital

- Working capital is an indicator of how much assets are available to be put to use in the business.

Ratios

Book value (BV) of common stock (CS) = $\dfrac{\text{Net stockholders' equity}}{\text{Net outstanding CS}}$

The book value of common stock represents the book value of common stock.

    Total Stockholders' equity $$.$$
Less: Preferred stock $$.$$
Less: PS dividends $$.$$
Less: <u>Liquidating dividends</u> $$.$$
   Net Stockholder's Equity $$.$$

$\dfrac{\text{CS \$\$}}{\text{CS Par value}}$ = C.S. Shares

            CS Shares
            Less: <u>TS Shares</u>
                Net O/s CS

BV of CS = $\dfrac{\text{Net Stockholder's Equity}}{\text{Net O/s CS}}$

Liquidity Ratios

Current ratio = $\dfrac{\text{Current asset}}{\text{Current liabilities}}$

Current ratio is an indicator of current assets to current liabilities. For example, a ratio of 1.5 indicates there are 1½ more assets than liabilities.
Not all items in the numerator and dominator are readily convertible to dash.

Quick ratio = $\dfrac{\text{Cash + Accounts receivable + Inventory}}{\text{Current liabilities}}$

Quick ratio assets are readily convertible to cash to pay liabilities.

FINANCIAL STATEMENTS

Financial Statement	Notes Disclosure	Supplemental Info	Other Reporting	Other Info
Income Statement	Accounting principles	Changing prices	Management discussion and analysis (MD&A)	Discussions
Balance Sheet	Summary of significant accounting policies		Letters to shareholders	Analyst report
Cash Flow	Contingencies			Statistics
	Investing methods			Articles
	Number of shares			
	Alternative methods used			

Summary of Significant Accounting Policies
- A GAAP requirement
- Disclosure of accounting principles in the *notes* to the financial statements describes the
  - Criteria or basis used for certain line items in the financial statements.
  - Does *not* require the computations or details of the line item.

Multi Step—Income Statement

Sales
- Cost of sales (COS)
Gross profit (GP)
- Selling, general, and administrative expenses (SG&A)
- Depreciation
Operating income
Other income or gains   } nonoperating items
- Other expenses or losses   }
+ Unusual or infrequent items
Income before income tax
- Tax provision—(IBIT is adjusted for temporary and permanent differences)
Income from continuing operations - Net of tax   **EPS** reported
Discontinued operations – Net of tax   EPS reported
Income before extraordinary item
Extraordinary items—Net of tax—Unusual and infrequent   EPS reported
Net Income (NI)   **EPS** reported

Other Comprehensive Income (OCI) **Mnemonic: PUF D**
   Pension—MPL—net of tax
   Unrealized G/L (e.g.; available-for-sale marketable securities)—net of tax
   FC Translation adjustment—net of tax

Derivatives unrealized G/L (e.g.; cash flow hedge)—net of tax
Comprehensive Income - net of tax

Accumulated Comprehensive Income (ACI)
· The sum of comprehensive income.
· Reported in the stockholders' equity section of the balance sheet.

Earnings per Share (EPS)
· Must be reported for publically traded companies on the face of the income statement for the following items:
    · Income from continuing operations
    · Net income
    · Discontinued operations
    · Extraordinary Items **are optional**.
Nonpublic companies may choose to report earnings per share (EPS) but are not required.

Discontinued Operations
· Criteria for discontinued operation
    · To dispose of its operations.
        · A commitment to liquidate (sell) its assets.
            · Assets are revalued prior to sale.
            · The commitment to dispose of its operations marks the measurement date.
        · And settle its liabilities.
        · No significant management involvement after the sale.
        · Operations cease *after* the sale.
· Footnote disclosure is a description of the operation being disposed.
· Income statement
    · Discontinued operations is reported net of tax.
    · Earnings per share reporting is optional.
    · Restate prior year financial statements.

Calculate the Gain or Loss on Sale of Discontinued Operations
> Operating income/ (Loss)—Premeasurement date: Net of tax
> ± Operating income/ (loss)—Measurement date: Net of tax
> ± G/L on Sale of operations: Net of tax
> **Gain or loss—Discontinued operations**—Net of tax

· Gains are reported when they occur.
· Loss is recognized immediately.

Example:

Loss—*Net of tax*

Loss is recognized when expected in full in current year

	Actual 2010
Operating income (loss)	$-75
Operating income (loss)	
Gain or loss—Disposal	**0**
Gain or loss—Discontinued Operations	$-75

Example:tGain—*Net of Tax*

Gain is recognized when realized (incurred).

	2010	**2011**
Operating income (loss)	$-150	
Operating income (loss)		-140
Gain or loss – Sale Ops		**+250**
G/L Disposal	$0	+110
Gain or loss – Discontinued Operations	**$-150**	**+110**

Extraordinary Item—Net of Tax

- Report in the income statement - Net of tax.
- Extraordinary item is unusual **and** infrequent in occurrence.
- Earnings per share reporting is optional.
- Report in:
    - Footnotes to the financial statements
    - The face of the financial statements

Earnings Per Share (EPS) Calculation

$$\textbf{Basic (BEPS)} = \frac{\text{Net income less PS dividend + Bond interest—Net of tax}}{\text{Average shares}}$$

$$\textbf{Dilutive (DEPS)} = \frac{\text{Net Income less PS dividend + Bond interest—Net of tax}}{\text{Average shares + Dilutive shares}}$$

Examples of Dilutive Shares:

- Stock options
- Stock warrants
- Stock splits
- Convertibles securities
- Contingent shares

Basic Accounting Equation

Assets = Liabilities + Capital (stockholders' equity section)
Each section of the balance sheet is listed in order of liquidity from the most liquid to least liquid.
Below are some common items listed in the balance sheet.

Balance Sheet Format
Assets Section

Current assets
- Cash and cash equivalents
- Marketable securities
- Accounts receivable—net of allowance for doubtful
- Notes receivable current portion
- Interest receivable
- Unearned Income
- Inventory
  - Consignment inventory held for another is NOT recorded.
- Prepaid expenses
- Assets held for sale/disposal $\leq$ 1 year

Noncurrent assets
- Investments
  - Available-for-sale securities, held-to-maturity security, cash-surrender-value life insurance, investment in bonds, land held for future building site
- Fixed assets—net of accumulated depreciation
- Intangible assets—net of amortization
- Intangible assets not amortized; for example, goodwill
- Cash surrender value—life insurance

Other assets
- Assets held for sale or disposal > 1 yr.
- Sinking fund
- Advance to officers

Total Assets

Liabilities Section

Current Liabilities
- Accounts payable
- Notes payable
- Interest payable
- Customer deposits (advances from customers)
- Unearned income (for example, rent received in advance)
- Contingent liability

Long-term (noncurrent) liabilities
- Bonds
- Mortgage
- Long term debt
- Commitments

- Contingent liabilities

Total Liabilities

Stockholders' Equity

Stock
- Preferred stock
- Common stock
- Treasury stock

Paid in capital (PIC)

Additional paid in capital (APIC)

Retained earnings (appropriated, unappropriated, restricted)

Accumulated other comprehensive income (AOCI)

Noncontrolling interest

Foreign Currency (FC) translation adjustment

Total stockholders' equity (SHE)

Total liabilities and stockholders' equity

FOREIGN CURRENCY TRANSACTION

Foreign Currency (FC) Transaction

Convert the Foreign Currency Invoice
- Convert a foreign currency invoice to United States (US) dollar.
  - use the spot rate at transaction date (invoice date).

    US $ spot rate times foreign currency invoice amount = US $ amount

- Convert a US dollar invoice to foreign currency.
  - use the spot rate at transaction date.

    FC $ spot rate x US dollar invoice amount = Foreign currency $ amount

Paying the Invoice
- Recording the payment
  - May result in a realized foreign currency exchange gain or loss
    - Report this in the income statement as part of income from continuing operations.
  - Foreign currency exchange gain or loss is recognized if the amount paid is:
    - Receivable: payment < owed = Loss on foreign currency exchange. Paid less than owed.
    - Payable: paid < owed = Gain on foreign currency exchange. Paid less than owed.

Example – Foreign currency transaction

	Euro $			US $
		-----------------Spot Rates---------------------		
Purchase	0.95099	$\frac{1}{1.05154}$	=	1.05154
Balance sheet date	0.93481	$\frac{1}{1.06974}$	=	1.06974
Payment sent date	0.94945	$\frac{1}{1.05324}$	=	1.05324
Payment received	0.94678	$\frac{1}{1.05621}$	=	1.05621

Sale or purchase—Seller or purchaser:
US company purchase inventory costing 325,000e

Sale (Euros)		**Payable (US $)**		
AR	$325,000	Inventory	$341,751	= $325,000 euros x 1.05154
	Sale 325,000	AP	341,751	

Balance sheet date—purchaser

$325,000 x 1.06974 - $ 347,666

$ 341,751 Owed at purchased date

Less 347,666 Amount owed at balance sheet date

$ - 5,915 US $ Loss

Record the loss

Unrealized FC Exchange Loss $5,915
    Accounts Payable $5,915

Payment date - purchaser

$325,000 x 1.05324 = $342,303

$347,666 Amount owed at balance sheet date

Less 342,303 Amount paid

$ 5,363 US $ Gain

Record the loss

Accounts Payable $5,363
    Realized FC Exchg Gain $5,363

Record the payment

Accounts Payable $342,303
    Cash $342,303

Payment received—seller

$342,303 US $ x 0.94678 = $324,086 Euros

$325,000 Amount owed euros

Less 324,086 Amount received euros

$ 914 Loss on foreign currency exchange

Realized foreign currency exchange Loss $914
    Accounts Payable $914

Record payment—seller

Cash $324,086
    Accounts receivable $324,086

Foreign Currency—Overview Payment Date

Transaction	Payment vs. Owe	= FC Exchange G/(L)	FC Spot Rate	U$ Spot Rate
Receivable Euros	Paid < Owe	Loss	↑	↓
Payable US $	Paid < Owe	Gain	↑	↓

FOREIGN CURRENCY TRANSLATION

FASB 52—Foreign Currency Translation (ASC 830—Foreign Currency Matters) are the standards used for foreign currency transactions and translations.

Types of Currency
1. Local currency (LC)—the local currency of the country where the entity is located.
2. Functional currency (FC)—the main (economic) currency of the foreign country.
3. Reporting currency (RC)—the currency used in financial statement reporting.

Financial Statement Conversion Methods
1. Remeasurement—converts local currency (LC) to functional currency (FC).
2. Translation—converts functional currency (FC) to reporting currency (RC).

1. **Remeasurement of Financial Statements**
   a. Converts local currency (LC) to functional currency (FC).
      i. **Monetary items**
         1. Income statement
            a. Revenue and expenses—use weighted average spot rate.
            b. Remeasurement gain and loss recognition
               i. Reported in the income statement as part of income from continuing operations.
            c. Cost of sales —a historical roll-forward schedule is maintained to value cost of sales.
            d. Depreciation—based on historical rates of the associated asset.
            e. Net Income—a historical roll-forward schedule is maintained to value net income. And represents the build-up of retained earnings.
         2. Balance sheet
            a. Assets and liabilities—use month-end spot rate
      ii. **Nonmonetary items**
         1. Income statement
            a. Revenue and expenses—use historical spot rates.
         2. Balance sheet
            a. Assets and Liabilities—use historical spot rates.
            b. Stockholders' equity— use historical spot rates.
               i. Valued at the accumulative effect of historical rates used to value its components.
   b. Income statement

      i.   Income (revenue) and expenses—use the year-end weighted average spot rate to value income and expenses.

      ii.   Cost of sales—a schedule is maintained to value cost of sales.

      iii. Depreciation—based on historical rates of the associated asset.

  c. Balance sheet

      i.   Monetary items—use balance sheet date to value monetary assets and liabilities.

      ii.   Nonmonetary items—historical rates are used to value assets and liabilities.

      iii. Equity—valued at the accumulative effect of historical rates for the components of equity.

      iv. Foreign Currency remeasurement adjustment—schedule of historical roll-forward rates.

Example:

	Beginning inventory	- Historical spot rates
	Purchases	- Average spot rate
Less:	Ending inventory	- Historical spot rate
	Cost of sales	- accumulative effect

	Beginning retained earnings	- Historical spot rate
	Net income or (loss)	- Roll-forward historical rates
Less:	Dividends	- Historical spot rates
	Ending retained earnings—accumulative effect	

2. **Translation of Financial Statements**

  a. Converts functional currency (FC) to reporting currency (RC).

  b. Income statement

      i.   Income (revenue) and expenses—use the weighted average spot rate at period end.

  c. Balance Sheet

      i.   Assets and liabilities—use the month-end spot rate to value assets and liabilities.

      ii.   Equity section—use historical cost

         1. Common stock—valued using the spot rate at stock issue date.

         2. Additional paid in capital—valued using the spot rate at stock issue date.

         3. Retained earnings (RE)—the cumulative effect of net income to date.

         4. Foreign currency translation adjustment—the net change in foreign currency translation from one period to the next.

           a. Reported as other comprehensive Income.

Example:

	Beginning retained earnings	- Historical spot rate
	Net income or (loss)	- Roll-forward historical rates
Less:	Dividends	- Historical spot rates
	Ending retained earnings—accumulative effect	

Weighted Average Calculation

Weighted Averaged = $\dfrac{\text{Sum of the Monthly Spot rates}}{\text{\# of Months}}$

Example:

Spot rates 2017. 1 Euro = "x" US Dollars

	Euro	**US $**
October 31	0.910457	1.09835
November 30	0.942694	1.06079
December 31	0.949163	1.05356
January 31	0.934807	1.06974
	Total:	**4.28244**

$\dfrac{\$4.28244}{4 \text{ months}} = \$1.07061$ is the average spot rate.

$1.07061 is the average spot rate used to convert the income statement at January 31.
$1.06974 is the spot rate used to convert the balance sheet at January 31.

Example:

Net Income—roll-forward schedule

Example:	FC Euros	Yearly Average	US $
2014 Net income	55,000	1.21548	66,854
2015 Net income	46,000	1.09254	50,257
2016 Net income	50,000	1.05356	52,678
Balance Sheet—RE	**$151,000**		**$169,789**

Summary Overview

Income Statement	Remeasurement	Translation
Revenue	Average rate	Average rate

Expenses

	Remeasurement	Translation
Monetary	Average rate	Average rate
Nonmonetary	Average rate	Average rate
Cost of goods sold	Historical	Average rate
Depreciation	Historical	Average rate
Amortized—Intangibles	Historical	Average rate
Amortized—Deferred income tax	Average rate	Average rate
Amortized—Deferred charges	Historical	Average rate
Amortized—Bond discount	Historical	Average rate
Amortized—Bond premium	Historical	Average rate
Provision for uncollectible accounts	Historical	Average rate
Gain	Historical	Average rate
Loss	Historical	Average rate
Income from investments	Historical	Average rate
Or equity in earnings	Historical	Average rate

Balance Sheet

Assets	Remeasurement	Translation
Cash and equivalents	Month end rate	Month end rate
Marketable securities - equityanddebt	Historical	Month end rate
Receivables	Month end rate	Month end rate
Allowance for uncollectible	Month end rate	Month end rate
Inventory at cost	Historical	Month end rate
Prepaid	Historical	Month end rate
Refundable deposits	Month end rate	Month end rate
Property, plant, and equipment	Historical	Month end rate
Accumulated depreciation	Historical	Month end rate
Cash surrender value of life insurance	Month end rate	Month end rate
Deferred income tax assets	Month end rate	Month end rate
Intangibles	Historical	Month end rate
Goodwill	Historical	Month end rate

Summary Overview

Liabilities	Remeasurement	Translation
Payables	Month end rate	Month end rate
Accrued expenses	Month end rate	Month end rate
Deferred income tax liabilities	Month end rate	Month end rate
Deferred income	Historical	Month end rate
Long-term debt	Month end rate	Month end rate

Stockholders' Equity	Remeasurement	Translation
Common stock	Historical	Historical
Preferred stock	Historical	Historical
Paid in capital	Historical	Historical
Retained earnings	Historical accumulated	Historical accumulated
Foreign currency remeasurement adjustment	Roll forward—schedule	Not applicable
Foreign currency remeasurement translationa	Not applicable	Other Comprehensive Income

Example:

Month-end	Euro	US $
October 31	0.91046	1.09835
November 30	0.94269	1.06079
December 31	0.94916	1.05356

1/1/20XX	0.72539	1.37856
Current year average	0.94096	1.06275
Average for the period	0.93379	1.0709
Beginning inventory 12/31/XX	0.9153	1.09254

ABC Company acquired by ABC Holding Company, Inc. January 1, 20XX

ABC Company submits its financial information to ABC Holding, Inc.

ABC Holding Company, Inc. is a US-based entity.

ABC Holding Company, Inc. owns 100% of ABC Company.

ABC Company

December 31, 20XX

Balance Sheet

Remeasuremtent	Euros	Translation rate	US $	
Cash	15,000,000	1.05356	15,803,400	Monetary – Month end rate
Accounts receivable	4,500,000	1.05356	4,741,020	Monetary – Month end rate
Inventory	6,000,000	1.0709	6,425,400	Schedule
Land	1,500,000	1.37856	2,067,840	Historical rate
Building	4,500,000	1.37856	6,203,520	Historical rate
Equipment	3,000,000	1.37856	4,135,680	Historical rate
Total assets	**$34,500,000**		**$39,376,860**	
Accounts payable	4,000,000	1.05356	4,214,240	Monetary – Month end rate
Note payable	3,500,000	1.05356	3,687,460	Monetary – Month end rate
Common stock	2,000,000	1.37856	2,757,120	Historical rate
Additional paid in capital	3,000,000	1.37856	4,135,680	Historical rate
Retained earnings	22,000,000		23,270,538	Schedule
FC Remeasurement adjustment			1,311,822	Plug to balance
Total liabilities and stockholders' equity	**$34,500,000**		**$39,376,860**	

Income statement

Remeasurement	Euros	Translation rate	US $	
Sales	25,000,000	1.06275	26,568,750	Current year average
- Cost of sales	-18,750,000		-20,382,265	Schedule
Gross profit	6,250,000		6,186,485	
- Selling, general and administrative expenses	-3,750,000	1.06275	-3,985,313	Current year average
- Depreciation expense	-875,000	1.37856	-1,206,240	Asset historical rate
Operating Income/(loss)	1,625,000		994,933	
Other income/(expenses)	20,000	1.06275	21,255	Current year average
Inc. before income tax	1,645,000		1,016,188	
- Income Tax	-575,750	1.06275	-611,878	Current year average
Net income	**$1,069,250**		**$404,309**	

114

Remeasurement	Euros	Translation rate	US $	
Beg. Retained Earnings	21,180,750		23,140,817	Roll-forward schedule
Net Income/(Loss)	1,069,250		404,309	
Dividends	(250,000)	1.09835	(274,588)	Declared and paid 10/31
Ending retained earnings	**$22,000,000**		**$23,270,538**	

Roll-forward Schedule	Euros	Translation rate	US $	
Beg. Inventory	12,750,000	1.09254	13,929,885	Historical rate—period end
Purchases	12,000,000	1.07315	12,877,780	Weighted average rate—purchases
Cost of goods available	24,750,000		26,807,665	
Ending Inventory	(6,000,000)	1.0709	(6,425,400)	Weighted average for the period
Cost of goods sold	**$18,750,000**		**$20,382,265**	

ABC Company

December 31, 20XX

Balance Sheet

Translation	Euros	Translation rate	US $	
Cash	15,000,000	1.05356	15,803,400	Monetary – Month end rate
Accounts receivable	4,500,000	1.05356	4,741,020	Monetary – Month end rate
Inventory	6,000,000	1.05356	6,321,360	Monetary – Month end rate
Land	1,500,000	1.05356	1,580,340	Monetary – Month end rate
Building	4,500,000	1.05356	4,741,020	Monetary – Month end rate
Equipment	3,000,000	1.05356	3,160,680	Monetary – Month end rate
Total assets	**$34,500,000**		**$36,347,820**	
Accounts payable	4,000,000	1.05356	4,214,240	Monetary – Month end rate
Note payable	3,500,000	1.05356	3,687,460	Monetary – Month end rate
Common stock	2,000,000	1.37856	2,757,120	Historical rate
Additional paid in capital	3,000,000	1.37856	4,135,680	Historical rate
Retained earnings	22,000,000		24,002,575	Schedule
FC Translation adjustment			(2,449,255)	Plug to balance
Total liabilities and stockholders equity	**$34,500,000**		**$36,347,820**	

Income statement

Translation

	Euros	Translation rate	US $	
Sales	25,000,000	1.06275	26,568,750	Current year average
- Cost of sales	-18,750,000	1.06275	-19,926,563	Current year average
Gross profit	6,250,000		6,642,188	
- SGandA	-3,750,000	1.06275	-3,985,313	Current year average
- Depreciation expense	-875,000	1.06275	-929,906	Current year average
Operating Income /(Loss)	1,625,000		1,726,969	
Other income/(expenses)	20,000	1.06275	21,255	Current year average
Inc. before income tax	1,645,000		1,748,224	
- Income Tax	-575,750	1.06275	-611,878	Current year average
Net Income	**$1,069,250**		**$1,136,345**	

Roll-forward Schedule

	Euros	Translation rate	US $	
Beginning retained earnings	21,180,750		23,140,817	Roll-forward schedule
Net income/(loss)	1,069,250		1,136,345	
Dividends	(250,000)	1.09835	(274,588)	Declared and paid 10/31
Ending retained earnings	**$22,000,000**		**$24,002,575**	

GOVERNMENT ACCOUNTING

At-a-Glance View

Government Reporting

Management discussion and analysis

Government-wide financial statement

Fund statements

Notes

Supplemental info

Statistical data

Comprehensive Annual Financial Reporting

Introduction

Financial

Statistical

Economic Measurement and Accrual Basis

Measures economic resources available

Full accrual

Revenue - when earned

Expense - when incurred

Fixed assets—depreciated

Financial Statements

Government-wide Financial Statements

Propriety fund

Fiduciary fund

Current Financial Resources Measurement and Modified

Accrual basis (MAB)

Measures financial resources available

Government fund

Fixed assets and long-term debt are not recorded.

MAB

Revenue when measureable and available collected within 60 days of year end

Expense when incurred.

Record capital expense when paid.

Debt when due or matured. Interest and principle is recorded.

Government-Wide Financial Statements

Operational accountability

Economic resources

Accrual basis

Financial statements

Statement—Net Position

Assets

Liabilities

Deferred inflow (prepaid revenue)—Liability

Deferred outflow (prepaid asset) - Asset

Groupings

Government-type

    Full Accrual

    Fixed assets—Depreciated

    Infrastructure assets— roads, bridges, sewer, etc.

      Report net of depreciation and debt

    Modified Accrual Basis (MAB)

    Fixed assets—depreciated

    Infrastructure assets are not depreciated.

      And are recorded at cost.

Business Type

Full accrual

    Fixed assets—depreciated

    Infrastructure assets— roads, bridges, sewer, etc.

    Report net of depreciation and debt

Statement–Activities

Revenue

Full Accrual

Inter fund transactions are not eliminated between primary, business, and components.

Exchange—goods and services

Nonexchange—grants and contributions (capital and components)

Expense

    Full accrual

    Expenses include

      Interest on Long-term debt

      Depreciation on Capital assets

      Depreciation on Infrastructure

        assets.

Primary Government

1. State

Reporting units of the state government

General—state, county, and city—discrete

Components (blend)

Special purpose—parks, toll ways, school, and sanitation

Components (blend)

Discrete—separate legal entity

Managed by primary government

Primary government pays its major debts (not all of its debts)

2. Local

Reporting units of the local government

General—county and city—discrete

Components (blend)

Special purpose— parks, tollways, school, and sanitation

Components (blend)

Blend—separate legal entity—but does not report separately.

Financial activity is blended (combined) with the primary government reporting structure.

If omitted will create misleading financial statements.

Managed by primary government

Primary government pays all its debts

Accountability

The primary government is accountable for monitoring operations, funding, and spending of its government units.

Types of Primary Government Accountability

1. Governmental (operational)—measure the effective use of resources
2. Fiscal (fund)—measures funding, spending, and compliance with laws and regulations

Types of Government Financial Reporting

1. **Basic Reporting**
   A. Government-wide financial statements
   B. Fund financial statements
      1. Governmental
      2. Proprietary
      3. Fiduciary
   C. Notes
      1. Summary—accounting policies
      2. Description—reporting entity
      3. Cash and investment disclosure
      4. Fixed assets, long-term debt, pension, commitments, contingencies disclosure
      5. Disclosure—budget overages and fund deficits.
   D. D. Required supplemental information (RSI)
      1. Management discussions and analysis (MD&A)
      2. Pension schedules
         a. Funding progress
         b. Employer contributions
      3. Budgetary comparisons
      4. Schedule—supporting MAB reporting
         a. Modified accrual base (MAB) reporting

Governmental-Wide Financial Staements

Fund Classification	Reporting Basis	Alternate Method	Financial Statements
	Accrual	Modified accrual base (MAB)	Statement—net position
	Economic resources	Economic resources	Statement—activities

Fund Statements

Fund Classification	Reporting Basis	Major Funds (Mnemonic)	Financial Statements
Governmental	MAB	General D SCaP	Statement—Change in fund balance
	Financial measurement		Statement—Revenue, expense, and change. in fund balance

Proprietary	Accrual	IE	Statement—Net assets
	Economic resources		Statement—Revenue, expense, and net assets
			Statement—Cash flow
Fiduciary	Accrual	PAPI	Statement—Net assets
	Economic resources		Statement—Rev, exp, and net assets

Reconcile Fund Statements to Government-Wide Statements

Fund Classification	Reporting Basis
Government	Governmental
	Internal service
Capital expenditure vs. Depreciation expense	

Primary government
1. State
2. Local

Recording Budget - Revenue

Estimate revenue	$$.$$
Appropriation	$$.$$
Budgetary Fund Balance	$$.$$

Primary governmental activities
1. Governmental
2. Business type
3. Fiduciary type

(2) Types of government financial reporting
1. Basic
2. Comprehensive

(2) Types of primary governmental accountability
1. Governmental
2. Fiscal

Purchase order issued

> Encumbrance
> Encumbrance $$.$$
> Budgetary Fund Balance - Encumbrance $$.$$

> Encumbrance - records the request for a purchased item that has not been paid.
> When the item and Invoice is received record the actual expenditure.

> Record the actual expenditure

>   Expenditure $$.$$
>   Voucher payable $$.$$

> Reverse the encumbrance when the invoice is received

> Budgetary Fund Balance—encumbrance $$.$$
>   Encumbrance $$.$$

Government-Wide Financial Statements

Statement of Net Position

1. Full accrual accounting is used. Assets and liabilities, short and long term, are reported.
2. Economic resource measurement is used for reporting.
   A. Asset section
      1. Under full accrual accounting depreciation is recorded.
         a. Report capital assets net of depreciation.
         b. **Capital assets** are fixed and infrastructure assets.
            1. Fixed assets are property, plant, and equipment.
      2. Infrastructure assets—roads, bridges, sewer system, tunnels, etc.
         A. Infrastructure assets with an indefinite life are **not depreciated**.
         B. Infrastructure maintenance cost is **expensed**.
         C. Infrastructure additions and improvements are **capitalized and depreciated** over estimated useful life.
         D. Depreciation expense is recorded in the statement of activities.
      3. Under MAB (modified accrual base) accounting infrastructure assets are not required to be depreciated.
3. Capital assets, long- and short-term debt are reported in Government-Wide Financial Statements.
   A. Long-term debt is amortized.
4. Deferred revenue and expense
   A. Inflows and outflows are income and related expense from nonexchange transactions received in the current period, but are not earned or incurred for use until a future period.

Example:
2017 Property taxes collected in 2016 is a deferred revenue item. It has been collected but not earned.

Statement of Net Position - Format

	Governmental Type	Bus Type	Primary Government Total	Other Components
Assets Deferred outflows Liabilities Deferred inflows	Capital assets and infrastructure assets are reported net of depreciation.	Reports its own debt and capital assets.		

Statement of Net Position - **Net asset section** has 3 sections:
1. Invested in or Investment in capital assets (net of related debt).
   a. Only debt issued to finance the government capital asset is deducted.
   b. Long-term debt for other purposes or to finance capital assets not belonging to the government are reported in "other component" section.
2. Restricted section reports restricted contributions for use; for example, creditors, contributions, law/regulations.
   a. Expendable may be spent when due or condition is met.
   b. Nonexpendable are retained indefinitely.
3. Unrestricted

Statement of Activities

1. Full accrual accounting is used.
2. It is a consolidated financial statement.
   a. Governmental activities are the government fund activities
   b. Proprietary fund are internal service activities.
3. Interfund transaction are not eliminated between:
   a. **Governmental type** activities are supported through taxes and nonexchanges.
   b. **Business-type** activities are supported by providing goods and services.
   c. **Primary government and discrete components**
4. Expenses are reported by function.
   a. Full accrual accounting is used.
      1. Infrastructure assets are depreciated and recorded net of depreciation in the statement of net assets.
      2. Accumulated depreciation is recorded in the statement of net assets.
      3. Depreciation expense is recorded in the statement of activities.
         a. Under modified accrual base accounting is part accrual and cash basis.
            1. Infrastructure assets are *not* depreciated.
               a. And are recorded at cost in the statement of net assets.
            2. Accumulated depreciation is *not* recorded in the statement of net assets.
            3. Depreciation expense is not recorded in the Statement of activities.
   b. Infrastructure additions and improvements— capitalize.
   c. Infrastructure maintenance and extend asset life improvements are expensed.
5. 5. Revenue—recognized when measureable and available.
   a. a. Full accrual accounting is used.

    b.   Revenue is recognized when collected and expected.
   1. **When collected**
      a. Within the period.
      b. Up to 60 days after year end.
   2. **When expected**
      a. When accrued.
      b. Up to 60 days after year end.
    c.   c. Exchange revenue are goods and services transacted for payment.
    d.   d. Nonexchange revenue—contributions and grants (operational and capital)
   1. Four (4) Revenue programs—net of related functional expense
      a. Service charge
      b. Operating grants and contributions
      c. Capital grants and contributions
   2. Four (4) Categories
      a. **Derived**—sales tax, income tax, motor fuel tax, etc.
      b. **Imposed**—property tax, special assessments, fines, etc.
      c. **Government mandated—federal and state requirement**
      d. **Voluntary**—contributions from individuals to government entities/agencies
    e.   General
   1. Revenue

Statement of Activities—Format

Revenue	Programs	Governmental Type	Bus Type	Primary Government Total	Components
- Expenses		**Internal service fund** activity, **depreciation,** and **governmental fund** activity	Enterprise fund activity		
Change in position					
± Beginning position					
Ending position					

Fund Statements

Governmental Fund
1. Financial Resources measurement
2. Modified accrued base method used.
   a. Revenue—report when measureable and available (60 days after year end)
   b. Bond proceeds—report as "other financing sources"
   c. Infrastructure assets—*not* depreciated and *not* recorded in the balance sheet.
      i. Accumulated depreciation is *not* recorded.
      ii. Infrastructure assets are expensed.
      iii. And are recorded in the statement of Rev., Exp., and Chg. in fund balance.
      iv. Infrastructure maintenance is expensed.
3. Fixed assets and long-term debt is *not* reported.

4. Only reported in government-wide financial statements.
5. Governmental funds

	Mnemonic:	General D SCaP

Mnemonic	**Fund**	**Description**
General	General	Fixed assets are *not* capitalized in balance sheet. Fixed assets are expensed - statement of revenue, expense and change in fund balance. Capital lease is expensed *not* capitalized. Expenditure $$.$$ Other financing sources $$.$$ Financial statements. Long-term debt is not reported in balance sheet. General fund reports all financial resources except those reported in other funds.
D	**D**ebt Service	manages resources used to pay for long-term debt principle and interest. Payment of principle and interest is recorded when due *not* accrued.
S	**S**ervice Revenue	reports revenue restricted for a specific expenditure purpose revenue is recognized in current period if collected $\leq$ 60 days after period end
C	**C**apital Projects	reports financial resources restricted for the acquisition or construction of capital facilities and other capital assets reports bond proceeds used for capital expenditures record the bond revenue when received. reports grants received from state used for capital expenditures record grant revenue when received.
a	and	
P	**P**ermanent	reports interest (*not* principal) restricted for government programs. Principal remains in the account and interest is reserved for specific use.

Financial Statements

Balance Sheet	**Statement of revenue, expenses and change in fund balance**
Assets - fixed assets not reported. - Liabilities	Revenue - recognized when measureable and available. - property tax is available if collected $\leq$ 60 days after year.

Fund balance	Expense ————————————→	Expense - contains:
Nonspendable	Other Financing Sources	General
Restricted	Special Items	Debt Service interest expense relating to fixed assets - NOT capitalized.
Committed		Capital Expenditures (fixed Assets) - are expensed.
Assigned		
Unassigned		Other Financing Sources - contain:
		Transfers between funds
		Bond Proceeds - obtained from debt issue
		Sale of Asset Proceeds

Fund Statements

Proprietary Fund

1. Economic resources measurement
2. Accrual basis used
3. Fixed assets depreciated
4. Income determination and cash flow

   Mnemonic: IE

5. **Mnemonic: Fund**   **Description**

   I   **I**nternal Service   provides goods and service to the primary government.

   Reported as part of the consolidation in the government-wide financial statements.
   Capital lease expenditure is capitalized
   Fixed asset expenditure is capitalized.

   Equipment $$.$$
      Voucher payable $$.$$

   E   **E**nterprise   provides goods and service to the public. Enterprise services are fee based in nature.
   Capital lease expenditure is capitalized.
   Fixed Asset expenditure is capitalized.
   Examples of enterprise services: water utilities, airport, town swimming pool, etc.

   Equipment $$.$$
      Capital lease payable $$.$$

Financial Statements

Statement—Net Assets

Internal service is reported in a separate column

Assets ⎫ Current and noncurrent reported
- Liabilities ⎭ Current and noncurrent reported
Net assets
      Invested in capital assets, net of related debt
      Restricted
      Unrestricted

Statement—Revenue, expense, and change in fund balance

Revenue
Expense depreciation is reported.
Capital contributions
Transfers out
Change in net assets
Beginning net assets
Ending net assets

Statement—Cash flow

Direct method is acceptable

Operating
Noncapital financing ⎫
Capital and related financing ⎬ includes interest paid.
Investing ⎭ includes interest received.

      Capital and related financing includes
      Purchase capital assets
      Sale of bonds
      Capital contributed

Fund Statements

Fiduciary Fund
1. Economic resources measurement
2. Accrual basis used.
3. Services the government and public.
4. **Mnemonic: Fund**   **Description**

    P   **P**ension   manages employee retirements and other benefits

    A   **A**gency   Custodial in nature. Serves as an agent for the primary government

P	**P**rivate Purpose	manages funds used to benefit individuals, private organizations, and primary government
I	**I**nvestment Trust	Example: scholarship fund
		manages government investments

Financial Statements

Fiduciary Net Assets	**Statement—Change in Fiduciary Net Assets**
Assets	Additions
- Liabilities	- Deductions
Net assets	Change in net assets
	+ Beg.
	Ending net assets

INTANGIBLE ASSETS

Intangible Asset
- FASB 142 (ASC 350)—Goodwill and Other Intangible Assets
- Lacks physical existence
    - Example
        - Computer software
        - Patent
        - Copyright
        - Franchise
        - Goodwill
- Record at cost
- Useful life—20 to 40 years:
    - If known, amortize over expected useful life not to exceed 40 years
        - In some cases, the useful life may be renewed. See GAAP guidelines for details.
    - If unknown or indefinite, no amortization is required.
    - Goodwill is not amortized, but tested for impairment periodically.

Computer Software
- **For internal use**
    - Research and developmental stage
        - Expense cost
    - Product development and Implementation
        - Capitalize
            - Internally developed
            - Acquired (purchased) and internally modified
    - Post development and implementation stages
        - Cost is expensed
- **For sale**
    - Research (developmental stages) cost is expensed.
    - Product development and implementation cost is charged to cost of sales (COS)

Patent
- Amortize
    - **Utility and plant patents**—20 years from date of United States filing per US Patent and Trademark Office
        - Or 20 years from date of international application
            - Using the straight line (SL) method
        - Purchased patent is capitalized
            - Successful defense of a patent is capitalized
            - Unsuccessful defense is expensed
    - **Design Patent**—15 years $\geq$ May 13, 2015, per US Patent and Trademark Office
        - < May 13, 2015—14 years

Franchise
- Capitalize over the life of the franchise agreement using the straight line (SL) method
- Expense monthly charges.

Goodwill (GW)
- For GAAP is not amortized
  - Periodically tested for impairment.
- Tax—amortize—15 years

Copyright
- Protects original works of authorship
  - Useful life—author's life + 70 years per US Patent and Trademark Office
- For works created anonymously, pseudonymously, or for hire
  - Useful life lesser of:
    - 95 years from date of publication per US Patent and Trademark Office
    - 120 years from date of creation per US Patent and Trademark Office
- Per GAAP, useful life limited to 40 years
  - Renewal may be acceptable

Trademark
- A word, phrase, symbol and/or design that distinguishes and identifies a good or service
  - Useful life—none per US Patent and Trademark Office.
    - Depends upon its use
    - No set term as long as the trademark is being used, it does not expire
- For works created anonymously, pseudonymously, or for hire

Impairment
- A decrease in asset value of long lived and intangible assets
  - A decrease in asset value due to:
    - Use
    - Physical deterioration
    - Advance of technology
    - Obsolescence
    - Competition, etc.
- **Impairment Test**
  - Performed periodically or when circumstances indicate
  - Test: Undiscounted cash flow < Net book value: Impairment loss recognized
    - Impairment loss recognized = Net book value > Fair market value (Fair market value less net book value).
      - Asset is recorded at fair market.

INVENTORY

Abbreviations

Avg	Average
B-FG	Beginning finished foods
B-Inv.	Beginning inventory
B-WIP	Beginning work in process
B-QOH	Beginning quantity on hand
Chg	Change
COGM	Cost of goods manufactured
COGS	Cost of goods sold
COS	Cost of sales
DL	Direct labor
DM	Direct material
E-Inv.	Ending Inventory
E-FG	Ending finished foods
E-QOH	Ending quantity on hand
E-WIP	Ending work in process
FOH	Factory overhead
Inv.	Inventory
NI	Net income
QOH	Quantity on hand

Inventory Methods

- **Lower of cost or market (LCM)**
- **Retail**
- **Dollar value Last In First Out** is used to cost inventory pools
  - Similar groups of inventory items are grouped by class, category, etc.
  - The inventory pools are adjusted for changes in pricing.
- **Perpetual**—moving average
  - Recalculates unit cost prior to each sale
- **Periodic**—weighted average
  - Physical inventory taken periodically.
  - Weighted average unit cost is calculated based on all purchases for the period.
- **First In First Out**
  - Periodic
  - Perpetual
- **Last In First Out**
  - Periodic
  - Perpetual

Cost of Inventory

Includes

- Purchase cost
- Freight—in
- Insurance
- Warehouse or storage cost
- Other inventory cost
  - Handling charge—expense
  - Abnormal freight—expense
  - Interest on inventory—inventory loan—expense
  - Unallocated or unapplied fixed factory overhead expense
  - Fixed factory overhead—based on normal production capacity
  - Variable factory overhead—based on actual production for the period

Freight on Board (FOB) Shipping

- Risk of loss (ROL) passes when shipped
- Title passes when shipped
- Buyer pays shipping cost

Freight on Board (FOB) Destination

- Risk of loss (ROL) passes at destination
- Title passes at destination
- Seller pays cost of shipping

Accrue In-Transit Inventory

In-transit inventory $$

        Accrued liability $$

Record the Receipt of Inventory

Inventory $$

        In-transit inventory $$

Trade Discounts and Credits

Trade and credit discounts are deducted against purchase cost.

Example:

Purchase Cost: $50,000
Trade discount: 10% and 15%
Credit terms: 2%/15 Net 30
Deduct 2% if paid within 15 days.
Otherwise, the full purchase price is due in 30 days.
Shipping cost: $200

$50,000 Purchase cost
− 10% Trade discount ($5,000)
45,000
− 15% Trade discount ($6,750)
$38,250 Purchase cost net of trade discounts
− 765 Credit terms: 2%—15 Days
37,485 Amount due
+ 200 Shipping cost
$37,685 Total cost of Inventory

Methods for Recording Purchases

- **Gross method**
  - Records purchases at the gross amount
  - Records the discounts
- **Net method**
  - Records purchases net of discount
  - No discount is recorded

Record the Purchase Record the Purchase

Gross method

Freight cost $ 200

Purchases 50,000

(5000 + 6750 =) Trade discount 11,750

      Accounts payable 38,250

      Accounts payable 200

Net method

Freight cost $ 200

Purchases 38,250

      Accounts payable 38,250

      Accounts payable 200

If paid < 15 Days

Accounts payable 200

Accounts payable 38,250

    Credit discount   765

    Cash   37,485

    Cash   200

If paid < 15 days

Accounts payable 200

Accounts payable 38,250

    Credit discount   765

    Cash   37,485

    Cash   200

If paid > 15 Days

Trade discount 11,750

Accounts payable 38,250

Accounts payable 200

      Cash   50,000

      Cash   200

If paid > 15 days

Loss—Trade discount 200

Accounts payable 38,250

Accounts payable 200

      Cash   50,000

      Cash   200

Purchase Commitment

- A commitment to purchase
- Noncancellable obligation

- Is a noncancellable contract to purchase specific quantities of goods or services in the future at a fixed price
- Footnote disclosure
    - Description of the purchase obligation
    - Disclose projected purchases for 5 years
    - If the purchase commitment involves long term borrowing and redeemable stock disclose:
    - Maturities
    - Sinking fund requirements
    - Redemption requirements must also be disclosed
- Record purchase commitment losses
    - Occurs within the fiscal year
        - A loss accrual is recorded
    - Occurs after the fiscal year
        - A loss estimate is recorded
    - If the contract purchase price is greater than the market price, a purchase commitment loss is recorded.
        - Contract price ($25) > Market price ($20) = Loss purchase commitment ($5)

If the Purchase Commitment Loss is:
- Temporary—no action required
- Permanent—record the loss

Loss purchase commitment	$5	
Purchase commitment liability		$5

If Recovery ($7) > Recorded loss ($5)

- The recovery is limited to the recorded loss.
- Record recovery ($5) = Recorded loss ($5)
    - If the recovery occurs within the fiscal year.

Purchase commitment liability	$5	
Unrealized gain—Purchase commitment		$5

- If the recovery occurs after the fiscal year.
    - Prior period adjustment or accrual rules apply.

Purchase commitment liability	$5	
Retained earnings		3.50
Deferred tax liability		1.50 (Tax at 30%)

Or

Purchase commitment liability	$5	
Unrealized gain—purchase commitment		$5

Consignment Inventory

Consignor

- Owns the inventory
- Includes the inventory in quantity on hand
- When consignee sells the inventory
- Record Sale
- Revenue
- Receivable
- Commission expense

Consignee

- Does not include inventory on books
- Inventory is on loan for sale
- Consignee sells the inventory
- Record commission
- Revenue
- Receivable
- Consignment payable

Record shipment of inventory

Consignment Inventory $50,000
    Inventory   50,000

Record receipt of inventory - nets to zero in balance sheet

Consignment Inventory $50,000
    Accrued Liability   50,000

Sale—Consignment Inventory

Cost of sale $15,000
    Consignment inventory $15,000

Consignment receivable   25,000
    Consignment sale   25,000

Commission expense   2,500
Commission payable   2,500

Sale—Consignment Inventory

Accrued liability   15,000
    Consignment inventory   15,000

Consignment expense   25,000
    Consignment payable   25,000

Commission receivable   2,500
    Commission income   2,500

Inventory Declines—the market value of inventory declines. (Market Value < Cost)

If the decline is:
- Temporary no action is required.
- Permanent record the decline.

Example:

           Market   *$ 40.0*
           -Cost   *43.5*
      Inventory—Loss—3.5

    Inventory—decline market value   *$3.5*
        Inventory   *3.5*

Obsolescence

- Inventory has become outdated and materially diminished in value.

Record Obsolesce:

Inventory Obsolescence	$20,000	
Inventory		$20,000

- Loss is recognized when sold or discarded. The loss is reported as part of income from continuing operations.

General Overview—Account Interrelationships

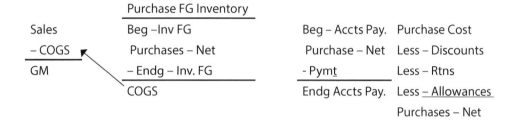

(FG = finished goods, COGS = cost of goods sold, COGM = cost of goods manufactured)

Manufactured Finished Goods Inventory

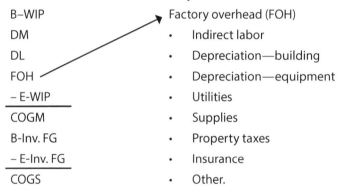

B–WIP
DM
DL
FOH
– E-WIP
COGM
B-Inv. FG
– E-Inv. FG
COGS

Factory overhead (FOH)
- Indirect labor
- Depreciation—building
- Depreciation—equipment
- Utilities
- Supplies
- Property taxes
- Insurance
- Other.

(WIP = work in process)

Over/Understated Value of Inventory

	B-Inv Understated			
		Was	**Should be**	**Chg.**
	B-Inv	$50	$100	($50)
	Purchase	200	200	$0
Less:	E-Inv	(150)	(150)	$0
	COS	$100	$150	($50)
	B-Inv	Understated	($50)	
	COS	Understated	($50)	
	E-Inv	Not affected	0	

B-Inv Overstated			
	was	**Should be**	**Chg.**
B-Inv	$100	$50	$50
Purchase	200	200	$0
Less: E-Inv	(150)	(150)	$0
COS	$150	$100	$50
B-Inv	Overstated	$50	
COS	Overstated	$50	
E-Inv	Not affected	0	

B-Inv Understated			
	was	**Should be**	**Chg.**
B-Inv	$50	$100	($50)
Purchase	200	200	$0
Less: E-Inv	(150)	(150)	$0
COS	$100	$150	($50)
B-Inv	Understated	($50)	
COS	Understated	($50)	
N	not affected	0	

B-Inv Overstated			
	was	**Should be**	**Chg.**
B-Inv	$100	$50	$50
Purchase	200	200	$0
Less: E-Inv	(150)	(150)	$0
COS	$150	$100	$50
B-Inv	Overstated	$50	
COS	Overstated	$50	
E-Inv	Not affected	0	

	B-Inv Understated and E-Inv Overstated			
		was	**s/b**	**Chg.**
	B-Inv	$0	$50	($50)
	Purchase	200	200	$0
Less:	E-Inv	(150)	(75)	($75)
	COS	$50	$175	($125)
	B-Inv	Understated	($50)	
	E-Inv	Overstated	75	
	COS	Understated	($125)	

	B-Inv Overstated and E-Inv Overstated			
		was	**s/b**	**Chg.**
	B-Inv	$100	$50	$50
	Purchase	200	200	$0
Less:	E-Inv	(150)	(75)	($75)
	COS	$150	$175	($25)
	B-Inv	Overstated	$50	
	E-Inv	Overstated	75	
	COS	Understated	($25)	

Inventory over and/or under stated relationship			
B-Inv.	**E-Inv.**	**COS**	**NI**
Understated	Okay	Understated	Overstated
Okay	Understated	Overstated	Understated
Understated	Overstated	Understated	Overstated
Overstated	Overstated	Understated	Overstated
Understated	Understated	Overstated	Understated

Lower of Cost or Market (LCM) Method

Selling price	$xxx.xxx
Less: Cost of disposal	
Net realized value (NRV)	xxx.xxx
Less: Gross profit	
Floor	xxx.xxx
Replacement cost	$xx.xx
Cost	$xx.xx

Step 1. Determine the market values—NRV, floor, and replacement cost.
Step 2. Select the middle value of market value—NRV, floor, and replacement cost.
Step 3. Select the lower of cost or market.

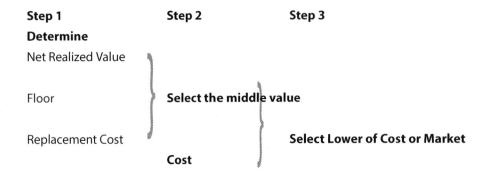

Step 1	Step 2	Step 3
Determine		
Net Realized Value		
Floor	**Select the middle value**	
Replacement Cost		**Select Lower of Cost or Market**
	Cost	

Example:

ABC Company sold $65 worth of widgets. Its cost of disposal was $15, and its gross profit margin was 10%. The cost of the product is $40. The replacement cost is $42. What is the value of ending inventory?

	Selling Price	*$65.00*
Less:	*Cost—disposal*	*-15.00*
	Net realized value (NRV)	*$50.00*
Less:	*Gross Profit*	*- 6.5 (at 10% of Selling Price)*
	Floor	*$43.50*

LCM Valuation Method

Step 1: Determine the NRV, floor, and replacement cost.

NRV	*$50.00*
Floor	*43.50*
Replacement cost	*$42.00*

Step 2: Select the middle range of NRV, floor, or replacement cost.

Mid-range cost of market	*$43.50*

Step 3: Select the lower of cost or market.

Market	*$43.50*
Cost	*40.00*

Therefore, inventory is valued at cost ($40).

Retail Conventional Method

		Cost		Calculate Cost / Retail ratio		Retail	
	B-Inv	180.00					250.00
	Purchase	1,020.00					1,575.00
	Markup						175.00
	Cost / retail ratio	1,200.00		60%			2,000.00
Less:	Sales						(1,705.00)
	Markdown						(125.00)
	Subtotal	1,200.00					170.00
	COS	(1,098.00)					
	E-Inv	102.00	=	60%	x		170.00

FIFO

		Cost		Calculate Cost / Retail ratio		Retail	
	Purchase	1,020.00					1,575.00
	Markup						175.00
	Markdown						(50.00)
	Cost / retail ratio	1,020.00		60%			1,700.00
	B-Inv	180.00					250.00
		1,200.00					1,950.00
Less:	Sales						(1,705.00)
	COS	(1,053.00)					245.00
	E-Inv	147.00	=	60%	x		245.00

LCM

		Cost		Calculate Cost / Retail ratio		Retail	
	B-Inv	180.00					250.00
	Purchase	1,020.00					1,575.00
	Markup						175.00
	Cost / retail ratio	1,200.00		60%			2,000.00
Less:	Sales						(1,705.00)
	Markdown						(125.00)
	Shipping						(20.00)
	Subtotal	1,200.00					150.00
	COS	(1,110.00)					
	E-Inv	90.00	=	60%	x		150.00

Dollar Value Last In First Out ($ Value LIFO)

- Values pools of inventory by adjusting for changes in pricing.

Step 1. Determine the cost index.
Step 2. Multiple the cost index times LIFO layer = LIFO layer value
Step 3. Add Beginning inventory + LIFO layer value = LIFO Ending Inventory value

$ Value LIFO

	E-Inv. Base	Cost Index	E-Inv. Current	$ Value LIFO
Beginning Inventory	0.00		0.00	0.00
LIFO Layer	LIFO Layer	Cost Index		LIFO Layer value
Ending inventory	0.00		0.00	0.00
LIFO Layer	LIFO Layer	Cost Index		LIFO Layer value
Ending inventory	0.00		0.00	0.00
LIFO Layer	LIFO Layer	Cost Index		LIFO Layer value
Ending inventory	0.00		0.00	0.00
LIFO Layer	LIFO Layer	Cost Index		LIFO Layer value
Ending inventory	0.00		0.00	0.00

Cost index x LIFO layer = LIFO Layer value

Example:

	B	C	C divided by B
	Ending Inventory	Ending Inventory	Determine
Date	**Base**	**Current**	**Cost Index**
1/1/2011	100,000	100,000	1.00
12/31/2011	130,000	136,500	1.05
12/31/2012	150,000	165,000	1.10
12/31/2013	135,000	155,250	1.15
12/31/2014	145,000	159,500	1.10

Answer

Date	Inventory Base	Cost Index	Inventory Current	$ Value LIFO
1/1/2011	100,000		100,000	100,000
Layer	30,000	1.05	**36,500**	31,500
12/31/2011	130,000		136,500	131,500
Layer	20,000	1.10	**28,500**	22,000
12/31/2012	150,000		165,000	153,500
Layer	(15,000)	1.15	**-9,750**	(17,250)
12/31/2013	135,000		155,250	136,250
Layer	10,000	1.10	**4,250**	11,000
12/31/2014	145,000		159,500	147,250

Inventory Relationships

	Perpetual vs Periodic
Ending inventory	>
QOH	Same
COS	<

	FIFO vs LIFO
Ending inventory	>
QOH	Same
COS	<

	Ending Inventory	QOH	COS
Periodic weighted	$5,713	3,500	$44,037
Perpetual moving average	$17,938	3,500	$31,812
Periodic FIFO	$18,875	3,500	$30,875
Perpetual FIFO	$18,875	3,500	$30,875
Periodic LIFO	$15,750	3,500	$34,000
Perpetual LIFO	$16,625	3,500	$33,500

Inventory ratios

Inventory turns = $\frac{\text{COGS}}{\text{Average inventory}}$

Average inventory can be calculated in different ways. Consistency is important for comparative purposes. One method uses the year-end inventory balance plus the current period balance to calculate the average. And cost of sale (COS) is on a year-to-date basis

Average days Inventory turns = $\dfrac{365}{\text{Inventory turns}}$

Example—Inventory Methods

Periodic—Weighted Average
Total purchases during the period divided by total quantity purchased during the period times the units sold during the period.

	QOH	Unit $	Cost	Ending Total $	QOH Ending
January 1	4,000	$4.50	$18,000	$18,000	4,000
January Sold	–2,000	$6.775	**-$13,550**	$ $ 4,450	2,000
February purchase	1,000	$5.00	$5,000	$ 9,450	3,000
March purchase	3,000	$5.25	$15,750	$25,200	6,000
April sold	–1,500	$6.775	**-$10,162**	$15,038	4,500
September purchase	2,000	$5.50	$11,000	$26,038	6,500
November sold	–3,000	$ 6.775	**-$20,325**	**$ 5,713**	**3,500**

Sold unit cost

January 1 beginning inventory	4,000 x $4.50 = 18,000
February purchase	1,000 x $5.00 = 5,000
March purchase	3,000 x $5.25 = 15,750
September purchase	2,000 x $5.50 = 11,000
	10,000 $67,750

$\dfrac{\$67,750}{10,000}$ = **$6.775 average unit cost of sale**

Ending inventory value:	$ 5,713
E-QOH:	3,500
Cost of sale (COS):	**$44,037**

COS: $13,550 January sale
$\quad$ 10,162 April sale
$\quad$ 20,325 November sale
$\quad$ $44,037 Total COS

Example—Inventory Methods

Perpetual—Moving Average
Recalculates average unit cost prior to each sale.

	QOH	Unit $	Cost	Ending Total $	QOH Ending
Jan 1	4,000	$4.50	$18,000	$18,000	4,000
January sold	−2,000	$4.50	**-$9,000**	$ $ 9,000	2,000
Feb Purchase	1,000	$5.00	$5,000	$14,000	3,000
Mar Purchase	3,000	$5.25	$15,750	$29,750 divide by 6,000 = $4.958	
April sold	−1,500	$4.958	**-$7,437**	$22,313	4,500
September purchase	2,000	$5.50	$11,000	$33,313 divide by 6,500 = $5.125	
November sold	−3,000	$5.125	**-$15,375**	$17,938	**3,500**

Ending Inventory value:	$17,938
E-QOH:	3,500
Cost of Sale (COS):	$31,812

COS: $ 9,000 January sale
 7,437 April sale
 <u>15,375</u> November sale
 $31,812 Total COS

Example—Inventory Methods

Periodic—FIFO
The first item purchased for the period is the first item out.

	QOH	Unit $	Cost	Ending Total $	QOH Ending
January 1	4,000	$4.50	$18,000	$18,000	4,000
January sold	−2,000	$4.50	**-$9,000**	$9,000	2,000

Use 2,000 of the January 1 beginning inventory at $4.50.

	QOH	Unit $	Cost	Ending Total $	QOH Ending
February purchase	1,000	$5.00	$5,000	$14,000	3,000

	QOH	Unit $	Cost	Ending Total $	QOH Ending
March purchase	3,000	$5.25	$15,750	$29,750	6,000
April sold	−1,500	$4.50	**-$6,750**	$23,000	4,500

Use 1,500 of the January 1 beginning inventory at $4.50. 500 remains for use against future sales.

	QOH	Unit $	Cost	Ending Total $	QOH Ending
September purchase	2,000	$5.50	$11,000	$34,000	6,500
November sold	−3,000		**-$15,125**	$18,875	3,500

November sold unit cost

January 1 purchase	500 x $4.50 = $2,250
February purchase	1,000 x $5.00 = 5,000
March purchase	1,500 x $5.25 = 7,875
	$15,125

Ending inventory value:	$18,875
E-QOH:	3,500
Cost of sale (COS):	**$30,875**

COS: $9,000 January sale
6,750 April sale
15,125 November sale
$30,875 Total COS

Example—Inventory Methods
Perpetual—FIFO
The first item purchased for the period is the first item out.

	QOH	Unit $	Cost	Ending Total $	QOH Ending
January 1	4,000	$4.50	$18,000	$18,000	4,000
January Sold	−2,000	$4.50	**-$9,000**	$9,000	2,000

Use 2,000 of the January. 1 beginning inventory at $4.50.

	QOH	Unit $	Cost	Ending Total $	QOH Ending
February purchase	1,000	$5.00	$5,000	$14,000	3,000
March purchase	3,000	$5.25	$15,750	$29,750	6,000
April sold	−1,500	$4.50	**-$6,750**	$23,000	4,500

Use 1,500 of the January. 1 beginning inventory at $4.50. 500 remains for use against future sales.

September purchase	2,000	$5.50	$11,000	$34,000	6,500
November sold	−3,000		**-$15,125**	$18,875	3,500

November sold unit cost

January 1 purchase	500 x $4.50 = $2,250
February purchase	1,000 x $5.00 = 5,000
March purchase	1,500 x $5.25 = 7,875
	$15,125

Ending Inventory value:	$18,875
E-QOH:	3,500
Cost of sale (COS):	**$30,875**

COS: $9,000 January sale
6,750 April sale
15,125 November sale
$30,875 Total COS

Example—Inventory Methods
Periodic—LIFO
The last item purchased during the period is the first item out.

	QOH	Unit $	Cost	Ending Total $	QOH Ending
January 1	4,000	$4.50	$18,000	$18,000	4,000
January sold	−2,000	$5.50	**-$11,000**	$7,000	2,000 = 4,000 — 2,000

Use 2,000 of the September purchase at $5.50. Zero purchases remaining.

February purchase	1,000	$5.00	$5,000	$12,000	3,000 = 2,000 +1,000
March purchase	3,000	$5.25	$15,750	$27,750	6,000 = 3,000 + 3,000
April sold	−1,500	$5.25	**-$7,875**	$19,875	4,500 = 6,000 — 1,500

Use 1,500 of the March purchase at $5.25. 1,500 remains for use against future sales.

September purchase	2,000	$5.50	$11,000	$30,875	6,500 = 4,500 + 2,000
November sold	−3,000		-$15,125	$15,750	3,500 = 6,500 -3,000

November sold unit cost

March purchase	1,500 x $5.25 = $7,875
February purchase	1,000 x $5.00 = 5,000
January purchase	500 x $4.50 = 2,250
	$15,125

Ending Inventory value:	$15,750
E-QOH:	3,500
Cost of Sale (COS):	$34,000

COS: $11,000 January sale
   7,875 April sale
   15,125 November sale
   $34,000 Total COS

Example—Inventory Methods

Perpetual—LIFO
The last item purchased prior to each is the first item out.

	QOH	Unit $	Cost	Ending Total $	QOH Ending
January 1	4,000	$4.50	$18,000	$18,000	4,000
January sold	–2,000	$4.50	**-$9,000**	$9,000	2,000 = 4,000—2,000

Use 2,000 of the January 1 purchase at $4.50. Zero purchases remaining.

February purchase	1,000	$5.00	$5,000	$14,000	3,000 = 2,000 +1,000
March purchase	3,000	$5.25	$15,750	$29,750	6,000 = 3,000 + 3,000
April sold	-1,500	$5.25	**-$7,875**	$21,875	4,500 = 6,000—1,500

Use 1,500 of the March purchase at $5.25. 1,500 remains for use against future sales.

September purchase	2,000	$5.50	$11,000	$32,875	6,500 = 4,500 + 2,000
November sold	–3,000		**-$16,250**	**$16,625**	**3,500** = 6,500 -3,000

November sold unit cost

September purchase	*2,000 x $5.50 = $11,000*
March purchase	*1,000 x $5.25 = <u>5,250</u>*
	$16,250

Ending inventory value:	*$16,625*
E-QOH:	*3,500*
Cost of sale (COS):	**$33,500**

COS: *$9,000 January sale*
7,875 April sale
<u>*16,625*</u> *November sale*
$33,500 Total COS

INVESTMENTS—CASH SURRENDER VALUE LIFE INSURANCE

Life Insurance Cash Surrender Value (CSV)

- Increases over the life of the insurance policy.
- Represents the value of insurance policy, if cashed in.
  - The initial years may have nominal CSV.
- For purposes of reporting, the CSV offsets insurance expense.

Example:

Insurance Premium $15
                                 -CSV - 6
Net insurance expense $ 9

Recording CSV

Insurance expense $9
CSV   6
        Cash $15

INVESTMENTS—COST AND EQUITY METHOD

Investor's Ownership Interest in Investee

Ownership Interest	Reporting Method	Control	Type of Investment
< 20%	Cost	Economic	Trading and Available for sale securities
20—50%	Equity	Significant influence	Equity securities
> 50%	Purchase	Control	Equity securities

- Economic—a financial invested interest.
- Significant influence—the ability to influence management and control operations.
- Control—has a 50% or more ownership interest in the voting stock of the company. Entity reports using consolidated financial statements.

Cost Method
- Used when there is < 20% Ownership interest in the equity of an investee.
- Recorded at the purchase price of the investment as a noncurrent asset in the balance sheet.
- If the investor can exercise significant influence over investee, the equity method should be used to record the transaction.

Recording a Purchase under the Cost Method

Record purchase price

Investment in corporate stock	$.$$	
Cash		$.$$

Record dividend income

Cash	$.$$	
Dividend Income		$.$$

Equity Method
- Used when there is ≥ 20—50% Ownership interest in the equity of an investee
- Recorded at the purchase price of the equity investment as a noncurrent asset in the balance sheet.
- The fair value (FV) over book value (BV) of the acquired assets are reported.
- Goodwill or negative goodwill is recognized.
    - Is not amortized.
    - But, tested periodically for impairment.
    - Negative goodwill is a return of capital.
- If the equity ownership lacks significant influence the cost method should be used.

Recording a Purchase under the Equity Method

Record purchase price

Investment in corporate stock	$.$$
Cash	$.$$

Record income from investment

Investment in corporate	$.$$
Income from investment	$.$$

(Alternate term for income from investment is equity in earnings)

Record dividend income

Cash	$.$$
Investment in corporate stock	$.$$

Record Amortization of FV over BV of related assets

Income from investment or equity in earnings	$.$$
Investment in corporate stock	$.$$

Converting an Investment from Cost to Equity Method

Convert Cost	to	**Equity Method**
2017—1/1		*2017—1/1*
Purchased—10% of ABC stock at $50		Purchase an additional 20% at $150
		(Total ownership interest in ABC stock is 30%.)

12/31 ABC income and dividend distribution

Net income 500= not applicable
         x 10%
Dividend   150   = 15

12/31

Net income   575   = $172.5
                     x 30%
Dividend   200   = 60

1/1 **Record purchase**

Investment in ABC stock	$50
Cash	50

1/1 **Record purchase**

Investment in ABC stock	$150
Cash	150

Total amount of investment in ABC stock
$50 + 150 = $200
Original purchase + additional purchase

12/31 **Record dividend income**

Cash	$15
Dividend income	15

12/31 **Record income from investment**

Investment in ABC stock	$172.50
Income from Investment	172.50

12/31 **Record Dividend Income**

Cash	$60	
Investment in ABC stock		60

- Restate prior year financial statements using the equity method as if always had been used.

Calculate prior year income and dividend distribution

Net income 500	= $50	
	x 10%	
Dividend 150	= -15	
	$35	
2017 Tax rate:	x 30%	
	$ 10.5 Deferred tax liability	

Record prior year income and dividend distribution

1/1 Investment in ABC stock	$35	
Retained earnings		24.5
Deferred tax liability		10.5

INVESTMENTS—SECURITIES

Types of Investment
1. Trading
2. Available for sale
3. Held to maturity

Method of Recording Investment
- Cost method
- Equity method

Type of Securities

Debt Security
- Corporate debt
- Convertible bond
- US treasury bond
- Municipal bond

Equity Security
- CS—common stock
- PS—preferred stock
- TS—treasury stock
- Stock—rights
- Stock—warrants
- Stock—options

Type	Life	Status	Carrying Amount	Type of Security	Balance Sheet classification	Cash flow classification	Unrealized gain or loss	Realized gain or loss
Trading	≤ 1 year	Selling	Fair value	Debt or equity	Current	Operating	Income from continuing operations	Income from continuing operations
Available for sale	> 1 year	Selling in the future	Fair value	Debt or equity	Current and long term	Investing	Income from continuing operations or other comprehensive income	Income from continuing operations
Held to maturity	> 1 year	Held	Book value	Debt	Current and long term	Investing		Income from continuing operations

Types of Investment

1. **Trading**
   a. Short term debt or equity security intended to be sold within a year
      i. Classified in the balance sheet as a current asset at fair market value
      ii. Represented in the cash flow statement in the operating section.
   b. Temporary changes in the market value of a trading security during the period are reported as unrealized gain or loss as part of income from continuing operations in the other income and expense section.
   c. Realized gain or loss are recognized when sold or disposed in the other income and expense section of the income statement.
2. **Available for Sale** (AFS)
   a. Debt or equity security is recorded at the purchase price.
      i. Represents a security that is not trading or held to maturity.
      ii. Classified in the balance sheet as a current and long-term asset.
      iii. Recorded at fair market value.
   b. Represented in the statement of cash flow investing section.
   c. Temporary changes in available for sale security during the period are recorded as an unrealized gain or loss in the other comprehensive income section.
      i. Net of tax in the balance sheet of stockholders' equity as accumulated comprehensive income.
   d. Later, when the security is sold, the unrealized gain or loss is reported in the accumulated comprehensive income of the balance sheet and is reclassified to the income statement as a realized gain or loss, part of income from continuing operations.
   e. Interest income is recognized in the income statement when earned.
      i. Does not decrease available-for-sale investment account.
   f. Dividend income is recognized in the income statement when earned.
      i. Does not decrease available-for-sale investment account.
   g. Permanent declines in the market value during the period are recorded as an allowance for decline in marketable security.

   Allowance decline in marketable security $$.$$
       Available-for-sale investment $$.$$

      i. Subsequent recovery of a permanent decline is disallowed, and no journal entry is recorded to reverse the decline
   h. If the fair value is elected, record available-for-sale security at face value.
      i. The debt or equity security is recorded at face value.
      ii. Unrealized gains and losses are recognized in the income statement as part of income from continuing operations in other income and expense section, and *not* as other comprehensive income.

Example:
Available-for-Sale Security *(AFS)*

2017 1/1	*Purchase cost*	*$20*	
2017 12/31	*Fair market value*	*25*	*+$5 Unrealized Gain—OCI*
	comprehensive income		*+5 Unrealized Gain—OCI* = *+11 Accumulated other*
2018 12/31	*Fair market value*	*30*	
			-$3 Unrealized Loss—OCI
2019 12/31	*Fair market value*	*27*	*+4 Unrealized gain—other comprehensive income*
2020 12/31	*FMV*	*31*	*$11 Accumulated comprehensive income net change*
2021 12/31	*Sold -*	*35*	*+$4 Realized gain*

Record Available-for-Sale Purchase 2017 1/1

Available-for-sale investment $20
*   Cash   20*

Record unrealized gain or loss

2017 12/31

*   Available-for-sale investment $5*
*   Unrealized gain—other comprehensive income $5*

2018 12/31

*   Available-for-sale investment $5*
*   Unrealized Gain— other comprehensive income $5*

2019 12/31

*   Unrealized loss— other comprehensive income $3*
*   Available-for-sale Investment $3*

2020 12/31

Available-for-sale investment $4
*   Unrealized gain—other comprehensive income $4*

Record Sale of Available-for-Sale

2021 12/31

Cash $35
*   Available-for-sale investment $31*
*   Realized gain $ 4*
Accumulated comprehensive income $11
*   Realized gain $11*

154

3. **Held to maturity (HTM)**
   a. A debt security is recorded at purchase price.
      i. Classified in the balance sheet as a current and noncurrent asset.
      ii. Amortized over the life of the debt using the effective interest rate method.
         1. Interest is recognized.
         2. Amortization of discount or premium is recognized.
   b. Unrealized gains or losses are not recognized.
   c. Permanent declines in market value are recognized as part of an allowance in decline of debt security.
   d. Premature sale of a held-to-maturity security is considered matured, if either condition is met:
      i. Sale occurs close to maturity date.
      ii. $\geq$ 85% of the principle has been paid or collected.
   e. If fair value method is elected, record the debt security at fair value market.
      i. Unrealized gain or loss is recognized in the income statement as part of income from continuing operations in the other income or expense section.

Reclassify Unrealized Gains or Losses
1. Reclass trading to available for sale
   a. Unrealized available for sale gains or losses are recognized in other comprehensive income.
   b. Unrealized gains or losses recognized under trading requires no reclassification.
2. Reclass trading to held to maturity.
   a. Unrealized gains or losses are not recognized for held to maturity securities not electing fair value method.
   b. Held to maturity securities electing fair value reports unrealized gains or losses as part of income from continuing operations.
   c. Unrealized gains or losses recognized under trading requires no reclassification.
3. Reclassification available for sale to trading
   a. Unrealized gains or losses recognized under available for sale are reclassified from accumulated comprehensive income to unrealized gains or losses as part of income from continuing operations.
   b. Unrealized gains or losses are recognized under trading and are reported as part of income from continuing operations.
4. Reclassification available for sale (AFS) to held to maturity.
   a. Unrealized gains or losses for AFS securities are reclassified from accumulated comprehensive income.
   b. And, are amortized over the life of the held to maturity security and reported in the income statement as part of income from continuing operations.
   c. Unrealized gains or losses are not recognized for held to maturity securities not electing fair value method.
   d. Held to maturity securities electing fair value reports unrealized gains or losses as part of income from continuing operations.
5. Reclassification held to maturity to trading
   a. No reclassification required because unrealized gains or losses are not recognized for held to maturity securities not electing fair value method.
   b. Held to maturity securities electing fair value reports unrealized gains or losses as part of income from continuing operations.
   c. Unrealized gains or losses are recognized for trading securities and are reported in the income statement as part of income from continuing operations.
6. Reclassification held to maturity to available for sale
   a. No reclassification required because unrealized gains or losses are not recognized for held to maturity securities not electing fair value method.

b. Held to maturity securities electing fair value reports unrealized gains or losses as part of income from continuing operations.

c. Unrealized gains or losses are recognized for available for sale securities as part of other comprehensive income.

LEASE ACCOUNTING

Types of Leases

1. **Operating**
   a. Recognized expense
   b. Record liability

2. **Capital**
   a. Recognized lease asset
   b. Record liability
   c. Types
      1. Direct financing
      2. Sales type

3. **Sale—leaseback**
   a. Operating
   b. Capital

4. **Leveraged lease**
   a. Not a direct financed lease
   b. Lessor financed the asset leased to lessee
      1. Lending company holds the title to the leased asset
      2. Lessor is responsible for payment to lender
      3. Lessee is responsible for payment to lessor

Initial Direct Cost

- Lessor
  - Cost associated with setting up the lease agreement: operating or direct financing
  - Amortized over lease term using straight line method
    - Sales type lease, expense initial direct cost
  - Examples
    - Broker or finder fee—the fee an individual or firm charges to arrange the transaction between the lessee and lessor
      - Amortize using straight line over life of lease
    - Appraisal fee
    - Processing fee
    - Closing cost
    - Commissions
    - Credit Investigation cost
    - Legal

Prepaid Rent

- Deferred charge
  - Lessee records an asset (prepaid expense)
  - Lessor records a Liability (unearned revenue)
- Recognize when incurred or earned

Lease Bonus

- Lessee pays lessor a nonrefundable bonus; for example; to obtain favorable lease terms.

- Deferred charge
  - Lessee records an asset (prepaid expense)
  - Lessor records a liability (unearned revenue)
- Recognize when incurred or earned
- Amortize using straight line method over life of lease

Lease Modification

1. Extend lease term—does not qualify as a new lease
2. Grants additional rights and use
   a. Qualifies as a new lease
      1. Record new lease as a separate lease
      2. Close original lease
3. Change from operating to capital
   a. Close operating lease
   b. Capital lease, record the asset and related liability
4. Change from capital to operating
   a. Capital lease, remove the asset and related liability
      1. Gain is deferred.
         a. Amortize using straight line over remaining asset life.
      2. Unless remaining asset life is < 25%. Then, gain is fully recognized.
      3. Loss recognized immediately.
   b. Operating lease follows operating lease rules.

Early Termination Fees
- Operating lease
  - Payable is settled.
  - Termination fees—expense
  - Lease payments—record accordingly
- Capital lease
  - Payable is settled
  - Asset is removed from books
  - Gain and loss are recognized
  - Termination fees—expense
  - Lease payments—record accordingly

Security Deposit

      Refundable Security Deposit (returned to lessee net of deductions in some cases)

Lessee records a receivable.

Lessor records a liability.

Lessee	**When paid**			**When refunded**		
	Security deposit	$$$		Cash	$$$	
	Cash		$$$	Expense (deductions)	$$$	
				Security deposit		$$$

Lessor	**When received**			**When refunded**		
	Cash	$$$		Security deposit	$$$	
	Security deposit		$$$	Fees		$$$
				Cash		$$$

Nonrefundable Security Deposit

Deferred charge amortized straight line over life of lease.

Lessor records unearned rent.

Lessee records prepaid expense.

Lessee	**When paid**			**Amortize**		
	Unearned rent	$$$		Rent expense	$$$	
	Cash		$$$	Unearned rent		$$$

Lessor	**When received**			**Amortize**		
	Cash	$$$		Unearned rent	$$$	
	Unearned rent		$$$	Rent revenue		$$$

Security Deposit Applied to Rent (Nonrefundable security deposit)

Asset—lessee

Liability—lessor

Lessee	**When paid**			**Amortize**		
	Unearned rent	$$$		Rent expense	$$$	
	Cash		$$$	Unearned rent		$$$

Lessor	**When received**			**Amortize**		
	Cash	$$$		Unearned rent	$$$	
	Unearned rent		$$$	Rent revenue		$$$

Leasehold Improvement
- Capital expenditure for land or building
- Capital improvements to lease property
    - Amortize over the lesser of leas term or asset useful life.
    - If the improvement is in lieu of rent, expense the expenditure.
- **Option to renew lease is uncertain**: amortize over the lesser of lease term or asset useful life.
- Option to renew lease is likely or certainty: amortize over the lesser of extended lease term or asset useful life.

Termination
- Real estate lease
    - Asset and obligation is removed from books.
    - Recognize gain or loss accordingly.
- Non-real-estate lease
    - Operating lease—debt settled and removed from books.
    - Capital lease
        - Asset and obligation is removed from books.
        - Recognize gain or loss accordingly.
- Termination fees
    - Operating or capital lease
        - Expense termination fees as part of income from continuing operations

Type of Lease	Lease Classification—Lessee	Lease Classification—Lessor
Rental	Operating lease	Rental
Sales type	Capital lease	Sales type
Direct financing	Capital lease	Direct financing
Sale—leaseback	Sale and operating or capital lease	Sale—leaseback

Lease recognition

Balance Sheet Recognition

At signing:	Lease book value at signing	
Less:	Payment at signing (if applicable)	
At signing:	**Ending lease payable**	x Interest rate x time = **Interest**
Plus:	**Interest**	
Less:	Payment	
Year 1:	**Ending lease payable**	x Interest rate x time = **Interest**
Plus:	Interest	
Less:	Payment	
Year 2:	**Ending lease payable**	x Interest rate x time = **Interest**
Plus:	Interest	
Less:	Payment	
Year 3:	**Ending lease payable**	x Interest rate x time = **Interest**

Current and long-term portion of the Lease

Current portion

	Lease payment
Less:	Interest
	Current portion of the lease

Long-term portion

	Ending book value
Less:	Current portion of the lease
	Long-term portion of the lease

Financial Statement Disclosure

Notes to the Financial Statement

- Lease
  - Footnote to the financial statements
    - Description of lease agreement
    - Terms of lease agreement
    - Minimum lease payments (MLP)—prepare a schedule for the first 5 years
      - Payments *after* 5 years may be expressed as total MLP for the life of the lease or the balance remaining on the least term.

Example:

 8-year lease $100 annually
   List the first 5 years—$100 payments
   Total lease payments—$800
       Or
   8-year lease $100 annually
   List the first 5 years—$100 payments
   Total Remaining payments—$300

Audit Lease Agreement
- Provide a copy of lease agreement
- Proof of purchase documentation—for bargain purchase options (cost verification)
- Monthly lease invoice—for proof of sale or expense (income or expense verification)
- Amortization Schedule—when applicable.
- Cash Receipt—as proof of payment. Validation of agreement.

Operating Lease
- Does not meet the criteria of a capital lease
- **Lessee**—Rent (lease) expense
- **Lessor**—Rent (lease) revenue
- Rent is
  - **Straight line** over the life of the lease
    - Fixed rent or lease payments remain the same **over the life of lease**

- Variable (uneven) rent or lease payments vary over the life of lease.
- Free rent is given as an incentive to the customer, no rent is charged for a certain period of time during the term of the lease.
- **Calculate straight line** lease payment

  Total variable rent payments

  - Free rent

  Net rental payments

$$\frac{\text{Net rental payments}}{\text{Lease term}} = \text{Rental income or expense}$$

Example: Straight line variable (uneven) rent or lease payments

Lessor purchased a building for $810k and depreciated it over 30 years and leased the building under a five-year contract with variable lease payments.

Lessor

Building $810

Mortgage payment $760

Cash $50

Depreciation (30 years)

Depreciation expense $27

Accumulated depreciation $27

5-year lease—office space—payment schedule.

Year	Payments
1	$10
2	10
3	12
4	12
5	16

Total: 60 $\frac{\$60}{5 \text{ years}} = \$12$ Rent or lease revenue/expense

Operating Lease

		Payable or **Receivable** Amount
	Beginning Balance—Rent Accrual	12,000
	Payment	(10,000)
Year 1	Ending Balance	**$2,000**
	Rent Accrual	12,000
	Payment	(10,000)
Year 2	Ending Balance	**$4,0000**
	Rent Accrual	12,000
	Payment	(12,000)
Year 3	Ending Balance.	**$4,000**

	Rent Accrual	12,000
	Payment	(12,000)
Year 4	Ending Balance	**$4,000**
	Rent Accrual	12,000
	Payment	(16,000)
Year 5	Ending Balance	**$0**

Lessor   **Lessee**

Receivable   Payable

Lease receivable $12 12 12 12 12   Lease expense $12 12 12 12 12

    Lease revenue $12 12 12 12 12   Lease payable $12 12 12 12 12

Cash receipt   Cash Payment

Cash $10 10 12 12 16   Lease Payable $10 10 12 12 16

    Lease Receivable $10 10 12 12 16   Cash $10 10 12 12 16

Capital Lease—Criteria
Capital Lease contains:
- A capital asset (lessee)
- A payable (lessee) or receivable (lessor)
- Current portion equals payment less interest due in $\leq$ 1 year.
- Noncurrent portion equals the payable or receivable balance less current portion.
  - Interest expense (lessee) or interest revenue (lessor).
- Classify lease agreement as a capital lease
  - If any one of the criteria applies, a capital lease is recognized (recorded).
    - **O O**wnership transfers at lease end
    - **W W**ith bargain purchase option (BPO)
    - **N N**inety %: present value (PV) of minimum lese payment (MLP) > 90% asset value
    - **S Seventy five %. Lease term > 75% asset life**
  - Depreciate the capital asset using the lesser of lease term or asset useful life.

Bargain Purchase Option (BPO)
- **Option to purchase** asset less than fair value at lease end.
  - Should be the lease payable or receivable balance at the end of the lease term.
  - Stated in the lease agreement.
  - Is recorded at the present value of 1 times bargain purchase option.
  - Record BPO as an addition to the present value of minimum lease payment.
- **If the decision to exercise is:**
  - Uncertain: amortize over the lesser of asset useful life or lease term.
  - Likely (Probable): amortize over the useful life.

Guaranteed Residual Value (GRV)
- Lessee guarantees asset value at lease end.
- 3rd party *cannot* guarantee asset value.
- GRV is recorded at present value of 1 as an addition to present value of minimum lease payment.
- GRV should be the balance of the receivable and payable at the end of the lease term.

- GRV is the asset book value at the end of the lease term.

Unguaranteed Residual Value (URV)
- Lessee does not guarantee asset residual value at lease end.

Minimum Lease Payment (MLP) per lease agreement.
- Due at the Beginning of period (BOP) is an Annuity due.
- Due at the End of period (EOP) is an Ordinary Annuity.

Interest is calculated
- **Implicit rate**
  - The interest rate stated in the lease agreement.
  - And known to the borrower.
  - Is used to calculate interest.
- **Incremental rate**
  - Borrower's credit rate
  - Used if the implicit rate is unknown

Calculating Book Value of Capital lease at Signing

PV of MLP = PV of ordinary annuity or annuity due x minimum lease payment
+ <u>PV of bargain purchase option, guaranteed residual value = PV of 1 x BPO, GRV</u>
Lease book value at signing

Balance Sheet Recognition

At signing:	Lease book value at signing	
Less:	<u>Payment at signing (if applicable)</u>	
At signing:	**Ending balance**	
Plus:	**Interest**	
Less:	<u>Payment</u>	
	Year 1:	**Ending balance**
Plus:	Interest	
Less:	<u>Payment</u>	
	Year 2:	**Ending balance**
Plus:	Interest	
Less:	<u>Payment</u>	
	Year 3:	**Ending balance**

Current and Long-term Portion of the Lease

Current Portion

	MLP
Less:	Interest
	Current portion of the lease

Long-term portion

	Ending balance
Less:	Current portion of the lease
	Long-term portion of the lease

Capital lease

Direct Financing

1. **Lessee** records a capital lease.
    a. Asset is financed.
    b. Record at present value of minimum lease payment using the net method.
    c. Asset is depreciated by the lessee.
2. **Lessor** records a capital lease as direct financing.
    a. Record as an installment sale using the gross method.
    b. Asset is leased to lessee.
    c. Payments are reasonably assured.
    d. Installment payments are recieved.
    e. No profit is recognized.
    f. Interest is recorded over the life of the lease.

Lessor uses Gross Method

Record lease at signing

Lease receivable	Gross amount	
Inventory (lease asset)		Cost
Unearned interest revenue or income		Delta

Lease receivable = Lease payment x number of payments

Lease Receivable

	Gross Amount	
Less:	Payment at signing (if applicable)	
at signing:	Ending balance	x Interest rate x time = **Interest**
+	Interest—not applicable (record separately)	
Less:	**Minimum lease payment** (MPL)	
Year 1:	Ending balance	x Interest rate x time = **Interest**
+	Interest—not applicable (record separately)	
Less:	**Minimum lease payment**	
Year 2:	Ending balance	x Interest rate x time = **Interest**

Lessor

Record Payment

Cash	MPL	
Lease receivable		$$

Record Interest

Unearned interest revenue	$$	
Interest income(revenue)		$$

Lessee uses Net Method

Record lease at present value at signing

Lease asset	Present value—Minimum lease payment
Lease payable	Present value—Minimum lease payment

Lease Payable

	Present value at signing	
Less:	Payment at signing (if applicable)	
at signing:	Ending balance	x Interest rate x time = **Interest**
+	Interest	
Less:	**Minimum lease payment**	
Year 1:	Ending balance	x Interest rate x time = **Interest**
+	Interest	
Less:	**Minimum lease payment**	
Year 2:	Ending balance	x Interest rate x time = **Interest**

Record Payment

Interest payable	$$
Lease payable	Delta
Cash	MLP

Record Depreciation

Depreciation expense	$$
Accumulated depreciation	$$

Record Interest

Interest expense	$$
Interest payable	$$

Example:
Minimum lease payment, guaranteed residual value
Lessee leases equipment for 5 years at 9% interest.

Lease equipment

Lease term—years	5		
Payment due	1-January		
Interest rate	9%		
Minimum lease payment	$15,000	x 4.24	63,600
Guaranteed residual value	$10,000	x 0.65	6,500
Present value of 1 at 6%,10yrs	0.65		**$70,100**
Present value—bargain purchase option	4.24		

Lease payments—gross	75,000 = $15,000 x 5 years
Guaranteed residual value	10,000
Lessor Obligation	**$85,000**
Lessee obligation	(70,100)
Unearned interest	**$14,900**

	Lessor		Interest Revenue		Lessee		9% Interest Expense
# of Payments				# of Payments			
	85,000	Receivable			70,100	Payable	
	(15,000)	1st payment			(15,000)	1st payment	
1	70,000	**Receivable**	4,959	1	55,100	**Payable**	4,959
		interest			4,959	interest	
	(15,000)	payment			(15,000)	payment	
2	55,000	**Receivable**	4,055	2	45,059	**Payable**	4,055
		interest			4,055	interest	
	(15,000)	payment			(15,000)	payment	
3	40,000	**Receivable**	3,070	3	34,114	**Payable**	3,070
		interest			3,070	interest	
	(15,000)	payment			(15,000)	payment	
4	25,000	**Receivable**	2,816	4	22,185	**Payable**	2,816
		interest			2,816	interest	
	(15,000)	payment			(15,000)	payment	
5	**$10,000**	**Receivable**		5	**$10,000**	**Payable**	
	Total interest: $14,900				Total interest: $14,900		

At Signing—Lessor

Lease receivable	85,000	
Lease asset		70,100
Unearned interest revenue		14,900

At Signing—Lessee

Lease asset	70,100	
Lease payable		70,100

Payment

Interest payable	4,959	
Lease payable	10,041	
Cash		15,000

Depreciation

Depreciation expense	12,020	
Accumulated depreciation		12,020

Asset Value	$70,100
Guaranteed residual value	(10,000)
Net book value	**$60,100**

Asset value	$70,100
Depreciation expense.	(12,020)
Depreciation expense	(12,020)
Depreciation expense	(12,020)
Depreciation expense	(12,020)
Depreciation expense	(12,020)
Depreciation expense	(12,020)
Book value (GRV)	**$10,000**

Example:

Minimum lease payment, bargain purchase option

Lessor

Lessee leases equipment for 10 years at 6% interest.

Lease Caterpillar equipment

						Amount
Lease term—years	10					
Interest rate	6%					**Amount**
Bargain purchase option	10,000	x	1	=		10,000
Minimum lease payment	60,000	x	10	=		600,000
						$ 610,000

Lessee

				Amount
Minimum lease payment	Present value—annuity due—6%—10 years	7.8017 x 60,000		468,101
Bargain purchase option	Present value—1—6%—10yrs	0.5584 x 10,000		5,584
				$ 473,685

Gross payments	$ 610,000
PV— payments	$ (473,685)
Unearned revenue.	**$ 136,315**

At Signing – Lessor

Lease receivable	610,000	
Leased Asset		473,685
Unearned Interest Revenue		136,315

Payment

Cash	60,000
Lease receivable	60,000

Interest calculated

Unearned interest revenue	24,821
Interest income (revenue)	24,821

Example:
Minimum lease payment, bargain purchase option

Lessor

# of Payments	Amount		Interest Revenue
	610,000	gross	
	(60,000)	first payment	
1	$550,000	**receivable**	$24,821
		interest	
	(60,000)	payment	
2	490,000	**receivable**	22,710
		interest	
	(60,000)	payment	
3	430,000	**receivable**	20,473
		interest	
	(60,000)	payment	
4	370,000	**receivable**	18,096
		interest	
	(60,000)	payment	
5	310,000	receivable	15,587

		interest	
	(60,000)	payment	
6	250,000	**receivable**	12,922
		interest	
	(60,000)	payment	
7	190,000	**receivable**	10,098
		interest	
	(60,000)	payment	
8	130,000	**receivable**	7,104
		interest	
9	(60,000)	payment	
	70,000	**receivable**	4,503
		interest	
10	(60,000)	payment	
	$10,000	**receivable**	$0

Interest total: $136,315

Example:

Minimum lease payment, bargain purchase option

At Signing—Lessee

Lease Asset	473,685	
Lease payable		473,685

Payment

Interest payable	24,821	
Lease payable	35,179	
Cash		60,000

Depreciation

Depreciation expense	46,369	
Accumulated depreciation		46,369

Lessee				**6%**
# of Payments	**Amount**			**Interest Expense**
		473,685	gross	
		(60,000)	first payment	
1		$413,685	**payable**	$24,821
		24,821	interest	
		(60,000)	payment	
2		378,506	**payable**	22,710
		22,710	interest	

	(60,000)	payment	
3	341,217	**payable**	20,473
	20,473	interest	
	(60,000)	payment	
4	301,690	**payable**	18,096
	18,096	interest	
	(60,000)	payment	
5	259,786	**payable**	15,587
	15,587	interest	
	(60,000)	payment	
6	215,373	**payable**	12,922
	12,922	interest	
	(60,000)	payment	
7	168,296	**payable**	10,098
	10,098	interest	
	(60,000)	payment	
8	118,394	**payable**	7,104
	7,104	interest	
9	(60,000)	payment	
	65,497	**payable**	4,503
	4,503	interest	
10	(60,000)	payment	
	$10,000	**payable**	$0

Interest total: $136,315

Example:

Minimum lease payment, bargain purchase option

Asset value	$473,685
Bargain purchase option	(10,000)
Net book value	**$463,685**

Asset value	**$473,685**
Depreciation expense	(46,369)
Depreciation expense	(46,369)
Depreciation expense	(46,369)
Depreciation expense	(46,369)
Depreciation expense	(46,369)
Depreciation expense	(46,369)
Depreciation expense	(46,369)
Depreciation expense	(46,369)
Depreciation expense	(46,369)
Depreciation expense	(46,369)
Book value (BPO)	$10,000

Example:

Calculating MLP

Lessor purchased Caterpillar dozer for $350,000.

Leased it to the lessee for 10 years at 6% interest rate. First payment due at January 1st signing.

Lease Caterpillar equipment		Lessor determines minimum lease payment	
Lease term—years	10		
Payment due	1 January	Cost of leased equipment	350,000
Interest rate	6%	GRV at PV of 1	(16,752)
Guaranteed residual value	30,000	**Asset net value:**	333,248
PV of 1 at 6%, 10yrs	0.55839		
PV of 1 Ordinary Annuity	7.80169	**Asset net value:**	$333,248 = $42,714.89
		Present value end of period	7.80169 MLP

Lessee records minimum lease payment at present value

MLP	$42,714.89	X	10	=	427,149
GRV					30,000
			Gross value of payments		**457,149**
			Lessee asset value		(350,000)
			Unearned revenue		**$107,149**

Example:

Calculating minimum lease payment

Lessee determines lease obligation

MLP	$42,714.89 x	7.80169 =		333,248
GRV	$30,000 x	0.55839 =		16,752
		Lessee asset and liability:		**$350,000**

Asset value	$350,000	=	35,000.00
Lease term	10 years		Depreciation expense

At signing Lessor

Lease receivable	457,149
Lease asset	350,000
Unearned interest revenue	107,149

Payment

Cash	42,715	
Lease receivable		42,715

Interest

Unearned interest revenue	18,437	
Interest income (revenue)		18,437

Example:

Calculating minimum lease payment

Lessor

# of Payments			Interest Revenue
	457,149	gross	
	(42,715)	first payment	
1	$414,434	**receivable**	$18,437
		interest	
	(42,715)	payment	
2	371,719	**receivable**	16,980
		interest	
	(42,715)	payment	
3	329,004	**receivable**	15,436
		interest	
	(42,715)	payment	
4	286,289	**receivable**	13,795
		interest	
	(42,715)	payment	
5	243,574	**receivable**	12,064
		interest	
	(42,715)	payment	
6	200,860	**receivable**	10,225
		interest	
	(42,715)	payment	
7	158,145	**receivable**	8,276
		interest	
	(42,715)	payment	
8	115,430	**receivable**	6,210
		interest	
9	(42,715)	payment	
	72,715	**receivable**	5,725
		interest	
10	(42,715)	payment	
	$30,000	**receivable**	

Total Interest: $107,149

Example:
Calculating minimum lease payment

At signing lessee
Lease asset   350,000
   Lease payable   350,000

Payment
Interest payable   18,437
Lease payable   24,278
    Cash   42,715

Depreciation
Depreciation expense   35,000
   Accumulated depreciation   35,000

Example:
Calculating minimum lease payment

# of Payments	Lessee		6% Interest Expense
	350,000	gross	
	(42,715)	first payment	
1	$307,285	**payable**	$18,437
	18,437	interest	
	(42,715)	payment	
2	283,007	**payable**	16,980
	16,980	interest	
	(42,715)	payment	
3	257,273	**payable**	15,436
	15,436	interest	
	(42,715)	payment	
4	229,994	**payable**	13,795
	13,795	interest	
	(42,715)	payment	
5	201,074	**payable**	12,064
	12,064	interest	
	(42,715)	payment	
6	170,424	**payable**	10,225
	10,225	interest	
	(42,715)	payment	
7	137,934	**payable**	8,276
	8,276	interest	

	(42,715)	payment	
8	103,495	**payable**	6,210
	6,210	interest	
9	(42,715)	payment	
	66,990	**payable**	5,725
	5,725	interest	
10	(42,715)	payment	
	$30,000	**payable**	
		Total interest:	**$107,149**

Sales Type

1. **Lessee** records a capital lease.
   a. Asset is sold to lessee.
   b. Installment payments are made.
      i. Record at present value of minimum lease payment.
   c. Asset is depreciated by the lessee.
2. **Lessor** records the capital lease as sales type lease.
   a. Sale of an asset.
   b. Installment payments are reasonably assured.
   c. Profit is recognized.
   d. Interest is recorded over life of the lease.

Profit is recognized

Sale price
Less: <u>Cost</u>

Or,

Present value—Minimum lease payment
Guaranteed residual value
Less: <u>Asset book value</u>
Profit recognized.

	Gross amount	
Less:	Payment at signing (if applicable)	
At signing:	Ending book value	x Interest rate x time = **Interest**
	Interest	
Less:	**payment**	
Year 1:	Ending book value	x Interest rate x time = **Interest**
	Interest	
Less:	**payment**	
Year 2:	Ending book value	x Interest rate x time = **Interest**

Lessor

Record lease at signing

Lease receivable	Gross amount
Cost of sale	book value of asset
Lease revenue	present value – minimum lease payment
Unearned revenue	delta
Leased asset	book value of asset

Record payment

| Cash | Minimum lease payment |
| Lease receivable | Minimum lease payment |

Record interest

| Unearned interest revenue | $$ |
| Interest income (revenue) | $$ |

Lessee

	Lease Payable	
	Present value at signing	
Less:	Payment at signing (if applicable)	
At signing:	Ending book value	x Interest rate x time = **Interest**
Less:	**Payment**	
Year 1:	Ending book value	x Interest rate x time = **Interest**
Less:	**Payment**	
Year 2:	Ending book value	x Interest rate x time = **Interest**

Record lease at signing

| Lease asset | present value – minimum lease payment |
| Lease payable | present value – minimum lease payment |

Record interest and depreciation

| Depreciation expense | $$ |
| Accumulated depreciation | $$ |

| Interest expense | $$ | |
| Interest payable | | $$ |

Record payment

Interest payable	$$	
Lease payable	delta	
Cash		minimum lease payment

Sale and Leaseback

This is a sales and leaseback of an asset.

1. **Sale**

	Selling price	
Less:	Book value of asset	
	Gain or loss realized	
Less:	Present value of minimum lease payments	
	Gain recognized	

a. Loss is recognized in full immediately.

	Loss realized equals loss recognized	
Less:	PV-MLP (not applicable)	
	Gain recognized	(not applicable)

b. Gain realized may be recognized or deferred.
   i. Gain recognition criteria:
      1. If present value of minimum lease payments (PV-MLP) is less than or equal to 10% of the leased asset at fair value, the gain realized is fully recognized.

	Gain realized is fully recognized	
Less:	PV-MLP (not applicable)	
	Gain recognized	(not applicable)

   2. If PV-MLP is greater than 10% of the leased asset at fair value and is less than 90% of the leased asset at fair value, the gain deferred is equal to the PV-MLP and is amortized over the life of the lease.

	Gain realized is partially recognized	
Less:	PV-MLP equals the deferred gain	
	Gain recognized	

   3. If PV-MLP is greater than or equal to 90% of the leased asset at fair value, the gain realized is fully deferred and amortized over the life of the lease.

Gain realized is fully deferred

Less: PV-MLP (not applicable)

             Gain recognized   (not applicable)

2. **Leaseback**
   a.   Follows operating or capital lease rules.

LONG-LIVED ASSETS

Long-Lived Assets

Intent to Dispose
- Sell or discard an asset: record at lower of net book value or fair value.
- Impairment loss recognized = Net book value > Fair value.

> Impairment loss $20
>   Accumulated depreciation $20

- Component of income from continuing operations
- Subsequent Recovery ($35) of a loss previously recognized ($20) is allowed.
- Record recovery ($35) < loss previously recognized ($20). The recovery is limited to the loss previously recognized.

> Accumulated depreciation $20
>   Impairment loss $20

Intent to Hold and Use
- The asset is retained and periodically tested for impairment.
- Test: Undiscounted cash flow < net book value: An impairment loss is recognized
  - Impairment loss recognized = Fair value < Net book value.

> Impairment loss $20,000
>   Accumulated depreciation   20,000

  - Component of income from continuing operations
- Asset is recorded at fair value.
- **Subsequent recovery** ($35,000) of a loss previously recognized ($20,000) is disallowed.

NONMONETARY EXCHANGE

1. **Elements of Nonmonetary Exchange**
   a. Property given
      i. Book value
         1. Known
         2. Unknown
      ii. Fair value
         1. Known
         2. Unknown
   b. Property received
      i. Book value
         1. Known
         2. Unknown
      ii. Fair value
         1. Known
         2. Unknown
   c. No boot
   d. Boot
      i. Given
      ii. Received

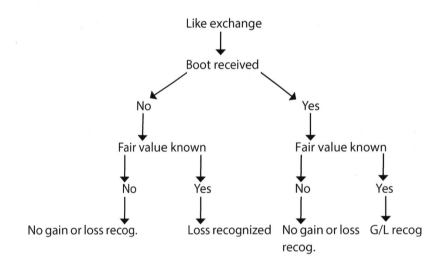

Nonmonetary Exchange
1. Involves
   a. Personal property
   b. Real property
2. Does not apply to
   a. Stocks
   b. Bonds
   c. Notes
   d. Convertible securities
   e. Partnership interest

    f.   Personal use property

    g.   Inventory

3. Per APBO 29 (May 1973)

    a.   A nonmonetary exchange has commercial substance if the entity's future cash flows are expected to significantly change as a result of the exchange.

4. Per Emerging Issues Task Force (EITF) 86-29 (Feb. 1987)

    a.   If boot (cash payment) is significant. It's a monetary transaction, not nonmonetary.

    b.   If boot (cash payment) is significant:

        i.   If boot $\geq$ 25% of asset fair value, it's a monetary transaction.

        ii.   If boot $<$ 25% of asset fair value, it's a nonmonetary transaction.

5. APBO 29 as amended by SFAS 153 (Dec. 2004)

    a.   Fair value asset given $<$ book value asset given:

        i.   Loss is recognized.

        ii.   Use fair value as the basis of the asset received.

    b.   Fair value asset given $>$ book value asset given:,

        i.   No gain is recognized unless boot is received.

        ii.   If boot is not received, the basis of asset received is the book value of the asset given.

1. **General Rule**

    a.   Fair value unknown

        i.   No gain or loss recognized.

    b.   No boot

        i.   No gain recognized.

        ii.   Loss recognized immediately.

    c.   Boot given

        i.   No gain recognized.

        ii.   Loss recognized immediately.

    d.   Boot received

        i.   Triggers gain calculation.

            1.   Gain deferred

            2.   Gain recognized based on the concept of "commercial substance"

    e.   Losses are recognized immediately.

    f.   Basis of property received can be determined by a journal entry

Gain Calculation—Personal Property

$$\frac{\text{Boot received}}{\text{Asset fair value}} \times \text{Gain realized} = \textbf{Gain recognized}$$

Gain realized

Less: **Gain recognized**

Gain deferred

Basis of Property Received

This can be determined by a journal entry.

Basis asset received	$$$ **plug**
Loss recognized	$$$ amount calculated
Boot received	$$$ amount given
Accumulated depreciation	$$$ amount given
Asset given	$$$ amount given
Boot given	$$$ amount given.
Gain recognized	$$$ amount calculated.

Accumulated depreciation / Asset given } = Asset net book value

Gain calculation—Real property

	Fair value asset given or received
	Cash received
	Mortgage—Old property
	Amount realized
Less:	Book value—asset given
Less:	Mortgage—New property
	Gain realized

Gain recognized = lesser of

    Boot

    Boot received = Cash received + Mortgage released

    or debt released = Old mortgage less new mortgage

    Or, **Gain realized**

Examples:

1. ABC Company exchanged an asset with a book value of $7,000 and gave cash of $500 in exchange for a similar asset valued at $6,000.

	FV	BV	Boot			
Given		7,000	500	**Deferred gain:**	**$0**	None. No gain recognized.
Received	6,000			**Loss recognized:**	**$(1,500)**	Fair value asset received less book value asset given less boot given
				Basis of asset received:	**$6,000**	Fair value asset received

Asset received	$6,000 (plug)
Loss recognized	1,500
Asset given	7,000
Cash given	500

2. ABC Company exchanged an asset with a book value of $7,000, fair value of $6,000, and received cash of $500 in exchange for a similar asset.

	FV	BV	Boot			
Given	6,000	7,000		**Deferred gain:**	$0	None. No gain recognized.
Received			500	**Loss recognized:**	$(1,000)	Fair value asset given less book value asset given
				Basis asset received:	$5,500	Fair value asset given less boot received

Asset received	$5,500 (plug)
Cash received	500
Loss recognized	1,000
Asset given	7,000

Examples:

3. ABC Company exchanged an asset with a book value of $7,000, fair value of $12,000, and received cash of $1,800 in exchange for a similar asset.

	FV	BV	Boot			
Given	12,000	7,000		**Deferred gain:**	$4,250	Gain realized less gain recognized
Received			1,800	**Gain recognized:**	$750	Gain recognized is prorated based on boot received.
				Basis asset received:	$5,950	Book value given less boot received + gain recognized.

Asset received	$5,950 (plug)
Cash	1,800
Asset given	7,000
Gain recognized	750

$$\frac{\text{Boot received } \$1,800}{\text{FV – Asset } 12,000} \quad \text{x} \quad \frac{\$5,000}{\text{gain realized}} \quad = \$750 \text{ gain recognized}$$

Gain realized	$5,000	FV – Asset	$12,000
'- Gain recognized - 750		'- BV – Asset - 7,000	
Gain deferred	$4,250	Gain realized $5,000	

4. ABC Company exchanged an asset with a book value of $8,000 and gave cash of $5,000 in exchange for a similar asset valued at $16,000.

	FV	BV	Boot			
Given		8,000	5,000	Deferred gain:	0	
Received	16,000			No Gain or loss recognized:	0	No boot received. No gain recognized.
				Basis asset received:	13,000	Fair value asset received less gain not recognized.

Asset received	$13,000 (plug)	
Asset given	8,000	
Cash	5,000	

NONPROFIT ACCOUNTING AND REPORTING

Private (Nongovernmental) Nonprofit Organizations

A nonprofit organization can make a profit as long as the profit is generated from the nonprofit purpose. The profits are tax free and may be used to expand the business, pay salaries, etc. Unrelated business activity is subject to federal and state tax based on certain criteria. Passive activity may or may not be subject to tax.

Type of Nonprofit Organizations

Religious	Churches, synagogues, temples, etc.
Education	Colleges and universities
Health	Health and welfare, research organizations
Social services	Libraries, sports clubs
Arts	Museums, performing arts centers

Restricted contribution
1. Relates to the contribution of an asset and how it is to be used.
2. Restrictions are externally imposed by donor or grantor.
3. Restrictions are *not* internally imposed.
4. A restricted contribution is not readily available for use when received.
5. Restriction classification:
    A. Time
    B. Use
    C. Purpose
6. Contribution:
    A. Variance power granted:
        1. The recipient of a restricted contribution granted variance power has the right to use the contribution as it sees fit.
        2. Contribution revenue is recognized.
    B. No variance power granted:
        1. The recipient of a restricted contribution *not* granted variance power does *not* have the right to use the contribution as it sees fit.
        2. The recipient serves as an agent for the donation.
        3. The recipient is to give the donation to a designated third party.
        4. No contribution revenue is recognized.
        5. A liability is recorded.

Example:

John Doe gives the Red Cross $20,000 to purchase a car for Mary Jane whose home and car were destroyed when heavy rain caused a mudslide in Southern California.

John Doe did not grant variance power to the Red Cross when he gave his donation. Therefore, the Red Cross must record the donation as a liability, and purchase the car for Mary Jane.

A donor makes a conditional promise to give (pledge)
1. Current year cash not received.
    a. Condition not met—no accrual recorded.

b. Condition met—record accrual at the present value of an annuity due or ordinary annuity as a temporary restriction unless it is permanently restricted.
2. Current year cash received.
   a. Condition not met—record a liability.
   b. Condition met—record accrual at the present value of an annuity due or ordinary annuity as a temporary restriction unless it is permanently restricted.

A donor makes an unconditional promise to give (Pledge)
3. **Current year** cash not received.
   a. Pledge is made record the accrual at the present value of an annuity due or ordinary annuity as a temporary restriction unless it is permanently restricted.
4. **Subsequent year** cash received.
   a. Record revenue and relieve accrual.

Financial Statements
1. Statement—financial position
   i. Is the balance sheet of a nonprofit organization.
      1. Current and noncurrent assets and liabilities are reported.
      2. Net assets are reported as unrestricted, temporarily restricted, or permanently restricted.
   ii. Cash contribution—record as restricted or unrestricted asset.
2. Statement – Activities
   i. Is an income statement or profit and loss statement of a nonprofit organization.
      1. Reports revenue, expenses, gains, and losses.
   ii. Cash contribution – record restricted or unrestricted revenue.
   iii. Functional expenses are recorded in the statement of activities and the notes to the financial statements.
   iv. Donated Services – record as unrestricted revenue and expense.
3. Statement - Cash flow
   i. Cash contribution
      1. Restricted contribution – record in financing section.
      2. Unrestricted contribution – record in operating section.
      3. Use of the cash contribution
         a. Record in operating or investing section.
4. Statement - Functional Expense
   i. Are used by
      1. Voluntary Health & Welfare Organizations
         a. Revenue and expenses are on a full accrual basis.
      2. Mental Health Associations
   ii. Functional revenue and expenses
      1. Revenue and expenses are reported by function.
         a. E.g., fundraising revenue and related expense.

Types of Health Care Organizations
1. **Private**—provides services in exchange for payment
2. **Governmental**—apply government accounting
3. **Voluntary health and welfare organization**—funded by voluntary contributions
   i. Statement of functional expenses
      1. Reports expenses by function and natural classification

Financial Statements
1. Balance sheet—current assets and liabilities reported separately.
2. Statement—operations
3. Statement—cash flow
4. Statement—change—net assets
   a. are classified as:
      i. Unrestricted
      ii. Temporarily restricted
         1. Capital contributions are reported.
      iii. Permanently restricted
         1. Capital contributions are reported.
5. Notes
   a. Charity
      i. Does not create a receivable or revenue.
      ii. Footnote disclosure required.

Statement—Operations
1. Performance Indicators reported separately
   a. Equity transfers
   b. Restricted contributions
   c. Contributions of long lived assets
   d. Unrealized gains and losses not restricted
   e. Investment returns restricted
   f. Extraordinary Items
   g. Discontinued operations
   h. Accounting changes
2. Patient services—use accrual basis—net of contractual adjustments.
   a. Does *not* include charity.
   b. Other revenue, gains, and losses include interest and dividend income, educational program fees, cafeteria meal sales, gift shop, parking

Statement—Change—Net Assets
1. Contributions restricted for long-term purpose are reported as:
      i. An increase to temporary restricted—net assets
      ii. Or an increase to permanent restricted—net assets
2. Expenses decrease—unrestricted—net assets
      i. Reports reported for depreciation, interest, and bad debt.

Colleges and Universities
1. Student tuition and fees revenue
2. Student graduate assistantships used for tuition are expenses

Financial Statements
1. Balance sheet—current assets and liabilities are reported separately.
2. Statement—operations
3. Statement—cash flow
4. Statement—change—net assets
   a. Net assets are reported as unrestricted, temporarily restricted, permanently restricted.
5. Notes

Statement—Change—Net Assets

1. Contributions restricted for long-term purpose are reported as:
    A. An increase to temporarily restricted—net assets.
    B. Or, an increase to permanent restricted—net assets.
2. Expenses decrease—unrestricted—net assets
    A. Are reported using their natural classification.
    B. Are reported for depreciation, interest, and bad debt.
3. Investment in debt securities are reported at fair value.

NOTES PAYABLE

The terms *liability* and *debt* are sometimes used interchangeably; for example, debt includes short-term and long-term loans, bonds payable, and other accrued expenses such as wages payable, income tax payable, etc. Accounts payable is a liability that represents an amount owed for a purchase on credit. A note payable is a written promise to pay and is also included in the liability category.

Debt is issued in exchange for:
1. Cash
2. Property
3. Goods
4. Services

Debt may be:
1. Financial in nature such as:
   a. Finance a purchase
      i. Auto
      ii. Bond payable
      iii. Note payable
      iv. Mortgage payable
   b. Obtain a loan
      i. Promissory note
      ii. Line of credit
      iii. Loan
2. Operating such as:
   a. Lease—auto, building, equipment, etc.
   b. Rent—auto, building, equipment, etc.
3. Debt is recorded at:
   a. Face amount if the debt is due $\leq$ 1 year.
   b. Present value (PV) if the debt is due > 1 year.
      i. Lump sum payment
         1. Is recorded at the PV of $1.
   c. Installment payments
      i. Are recorded at the PV of annuity due.
      ii. Or, at the PV of an ordinary annuity.
   d. Fair value if elected.
      i. No discount or premium is recorded.

Debt Overview

Type of Note	Interest Rate	Payment Method	Balance Sheet Reporting
1. Interest-bearing	Stated	Lump sum payment Installment payments	Current portion and Long-term portion
2. Noninterest-bearing	Not stated	Lump sum payment Installment payments	Current portion and Long-term portion

Noninterest-Bearing Note
1. Lump sum payment
    a. Due in ≤ 1 year is recorded at face amount.
    b. Due in > 1 year is recorded at the present value of 1.
2. Installment payments
    a. Due > 1 year is recorded at the present value of an annuity due or ordinary annuity.

Discounted Note
1. Relates to a note due in a lump sum payment.
2. Is discounted for 30, 60, or 90 days.
    a. The 30, 60, or 90 is used in the numerator to determine the discount.
    b. The numerator is divided by 360.
3. Is recorded at face amount net of discount.

$$\text{Face amount} \times \text{state rate} \times \frac{30}{360} \quad \text{or} \quad \frac{60}{360} \quad \text{or} \quad \frac{90}{360} \quad = \quad \text{Discounted note payable}$$

Interest-Bearing Note
1. Lump sum payment
    a. Due in ≤ 1 year is recorded at face amount.
    b. Due in > 1 year is recorded at the present value of 1.
2. Installment payments
    a. Due > 1 year is recorded at the present value of an annuity due or ordinary annuity.

Discounted Note
1. Relates to a note due in a lump sum payment.
2. Is discounted for 30, 60, or 90 days.
    a. The 30, 60, or 90 is used in the numerator to determine the discount.
    b. The numerator is divided by 360.
3. Is recorded at face amount net of discount.

$$\text{Face Amount} \times \text{state rate} \times \frac{30}{360} \quad \text{or} \quad \frac{60}{360} \quad \text{or} \quad \frac{90}{360} \quad = \quad \text{Discounted note payable}$$

Example:

ABC Company borrowed $100,000 on a 10-year, 7% installment note payable on January 1, 2017. The terms of the note require that ABC Company pay 10 equal payments of $14,238 each December 31 for 10 years.

1. Determine the principle payment at the end of the third year.   <u>8,286.79</u>
   It's an interest-bearing note. Payment includes interest.
   Ten equal payments would be $10,000.00. However, for this
   example, equal payments are $14,238.00.
2. Determine the note payable balance at the end of the 4ᵗʰ year.   <u>67,863.69</u>

                                                                          7%

Principal Payment	Interest Payment	Payment Total		Note Payment Balance	Interest
				100,000.00	
				(14,238.00)	
7,238.00	7,000.00	14,238.00		7,000.00	7,000.00
			Year 1	92,762.00	
				(14,238.00)	
7,744.66	6,493.34	14,238.00		6,493.34	6,493.34
			Year 2	85,017.34	
				(14,238.00)	
$8,286.79	5,951.21	14,238.00		5,951.21	5,951.21
			Y Year r 3	76,730.55	
				(14,238.00)	
8,866.86	5,371.14	14,238.00		5,371.14	5,371.14
			Yr 4	$67,863.69	
				(14,238.00)	
9,487.54	4,750.46	14,238.00		4,750.46	4,750.46
			Year 5	58,376.15	
				(14,238.00)	
10,151.67	4,086.33	14,238.00		4,086.33	4,086.33
			Year 6	48,224.48	
				(14,238.00)	
10,862.29	3,375.71	14,238.00		3,375.71	3,375.71
			Year 7	37,362.20	
				(14,238.00)	
11,622.65	2,615.35	14,238.00		2,615.35	2,615.35
			Year 8	25,739.55	
				(14,238.00)	
12,436.23	1,801.77	14,238.00		1,801.77	1,801.77
			Year 9	13,303.32	
				(14,238.00)	
13,303.32	934.68	14,238.00		934.68	931.23
$ 100,000.00	$ 42,380.00	$ 142,380.00	Year 10	$ (0.00)	

Example:

On December 31, year 1, Machine Company Inc. received a $10,000 note from two(2) separate customers.

For both notes, interest is calculated based on the

outstanding balance at an interest rate of 3% compounded annually and payable at maturity. The note from Boat Corporation is due in nine months. The note from Engine Inc. is due in five years. The market interest rate on December 31, year 1 was 8%. The compound interest factors are as follows:

Future value of $ I due in nine months at 3%   1.0225
Future value of $1 due in five years at 3%   1.1593
Present value of $1 due in nine months at 8%   0.9440
Present value of $1 due in five years at 8%   0.6800

Machine Company Inc. does not elect the fair value option for reporting the two(2) notes. At what amount should these two notes be reported in Machine Company Inc. December 31, year 1 balance sheet?

Boat Corporation   **$10,000**

Machine Company Inc. and Boat Corporation record the note lump sum payment due < 1 year is reported at face amount.

Engine Inc.   **$7,883**

Machine Company Inc. and Boat Corporation record the note lump sum payment due > 1 year is reported at present value of $1 compounded.

$10,000	x	1.1593	=	$11,593	x	0.6800	=	**$7,883**
Lump sum payment		Face value factor		Face value note receivable		Present value factor		Present value note receivable

Example:

A $25,000 8% loan paid over 5 years.

Payments are due at the end of the period.

Option 1: the payment includes principle and interest.

Option 2: the payment is principle only.

Determining the loan payment.

$$\frac{25,000.00}{\textbf{3.99271} \text{ is the PV Ordinary Annuity at 8\% for 5 periods.}} = 6,261.41 \text{ Option 1}$$

		Option 1	Option 2	8%
		Principal and Interest	**Principal Only**	**Interest**
	Principle	$25,000.00	$25,000.00	
	Interest	2,000.00		$2,000.00
	payment	**(6,261.00)**	(5,000.00)	
1	Balance	20,739.00	20,000.00	
	Interest	1,659.12		1,600.00
	payment	**(6,261.00)**	(5,000.00)	
2	Balance	16,137.12	15,000.00	
	Interest	1,290.97		1,200.00
	payment	**(6,261.00)**	(5,000.00)	
3	Balance	11,167.09	10,000.00	
	Interest	893.37		800.00
	payment	**(6,261.00)**	(5,000.00)	
4	Balance	5,799.46	5,000.00	
	Interest	461.55		400.00
	payment	**(6,261.00)**	(5,000.00)	
5	Balance	0.00	0.00	

Option 2, interest is reported separately.

Option 2, the payment amount is calculated by dividing $25,000 by 5 years.

Example:

Short term interest-bearing note payable

Borrowed $6,000 at 6% interest. Due in 6 months.

Record receipt of Cash

Cash $6,000
    Note payable—current $6,000

Recorded accrued interest—monthly

Interest expense $30 $6,000 x 6% / 12 = $30
Interest payable   30

Record payment of principal and interest at due date

Note payable—current $6,000
Interest payable   180   (after 6 months of accrual)
    Cash $6,180

Example:

Long-term note payable, interest bearing—lump sum payment

Borrowed $15,000 at 6% interest paid quarterly and principle due in 36 months.

Record receipt of Cash

Cash $15,000
    Note payable—noncurrent $15,000

Recorded accrued Interest – Monthly

Interest expense $75 $15,000 x 6% / 12 = $75
    Interest payable   75

Record interest payment at due quarterly

Interest payable $225   (after 3 months of accrual)
    Cash $225

Record payment of principle

Note payable—noncurrent $15,000
    Cash $15,000

OTHER COMPREHENSIVE INCOME

Net Income   Earnings per share is reported
Other comprehensive income (OCI)
Mnemonic: PUF D:

- **P**ension—minimum pension liability (MPL)—net of tax
- **U**nrealized gains and losses on available-for-sale marketable securities—net of tax
- **F**oreign currency translation adjustment—net of tax
- **D**erivatives unrealized gains and losses (cash flow hedge)—net of tax

Comprehensive Income (CI)—Net of Tax
- Measures overall financial performance.
- Includes
    - Some revenue and expenses reported in income statement
    - Gains and losses from nonowner activity
    - Unrealized gains and losses on available-for-sale marketable securities
    - Available for sale reclassification adjustments
    - Unrealized gains and losses on foreign currency translation adjustment
    - Changes in fair value of a derivative designated as a
        - Cash flow hedge forecasted transaction
            - Effective portion is reported in other comprehensive income
            - And later reclassified to earnings, when the forecasted transactions occurs.
            - Ineffective portion is reported in earnings.
        - Foreign currency hedge net investment in a foreign operation
            - Fluctuations in foreign currency is reported in other comprehensive income
    - Fair value hedge of a foreign currency transaction unrecognized firm commitment
    - Pension—minimum pension liability (MPL)
- Excludes
    - Prior period adjustments
    - Owner transactions
        - Investment by owners
        - Distributions to owners
- Other comprehensive income is reported in the
    - Balance sheet
        - Stockholders' equity section
        - As accumulated comprehensive income
            - is the accumulative effect of comprehensive income
    - Income statement
        - As a separate section following net income to arrive at comprehensive income
    - Statement of earnings and comprehensive income
    - Statement of changes in stockholders' Equity
- Notes to the financial statement
    - Disclosed in the
        - Summary of significant accounting policies.

PENSIONS

Balance Sheet

Pension Liability

		Overview

	Projected benefit obligation (PBO)	PBO
Less:	Fair market value (FV) of plan assets	Less: FV - Plan Assets
	Pension liability (PL) or **Unfunded PL** or **Unfunded PBO**	**PL**
+ or -	Net pension cost (NPC)	Less: NPC
	Additional pension liability (APL)	**APL**
Less:	Service Cost and/or Unrecognized prior service cost	Less: Svc Cost
	Excess pension liability (EPL)	**EPL**

Pension Liability (PL)
1. Prepaid (-) or accrued (+) expense
    a. If Projected benefit obligation > Fair market value of plan assets = Accrued expense
        i. Also referred to as underfunded projected benefit obligation
            1. a noncurrent accrued liability.
    b. Projected benefit obligation < Fair market value of plan assets = Prepaid expense
        i. equals an overfunded projected benefit obligation
            1. A noncurrent prepaid expense.

Record Pension Liability (PL)

Pension expense	$.$$	
Pension liability		$.$$

Recording Additional Pension Liability (APL)

Other comprehensive income	net of tax (less tax)
Deferred tax asset	Tax amount
Pension liability	Additional pension liability

Projected Benefit Obligation (PBO)

Beginning projected benefit obligation
+ Service cost
+ Interest cost = Beginning projected benefit obligation x discount rate
± Gain or loss on projected benefit obligation
Less: Benefits paid
Ending projected benefit obligation

Projected Benefit Obligation Gains or Loss
1. Gain (-) reduces the obligation.
2. Loss (+) increases the obligation.

Balance Sheet Activity

Plan Assets

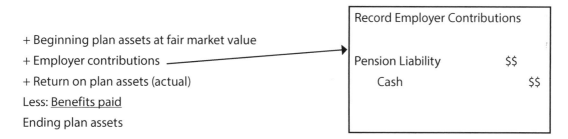

+ Beginning plan assets at fair market value

+ Employer contributions

+ Return on plan assets (actual)

Less: Benefits paid

Ending plan assets

Record Employer Contributions

Pension Liability	$$
Cash	$$

Actual vs. Expected Return on Plan Assets

Return on plan assets—actual (includes gains or losses associated with the plan)

Less: Expected return on plan assets

Addition to (+) or subtraction (-) from pension cost calculation

Expected return on plan assets = Beginning plan assets at fair market value times expected rate of return

Calculating the Benefit or Loss on Early Termination of Benefits

Lump sum payment (liability)

Annuity (installment) payments record at present value of the annuity payments.

Termination of benefits liability

Less: Savings on early termination of benefits

Loss on termination of benefits

Recording Early Termination of Benefits

Loss on termination of benefits	$$$	
Accrued pension cost	$$$	
Termination of benefits liability		$$$

Income Statement Activity

Pension Cost (PC)

Service cost = Change in projected benefit obligation

Interest = PBO x Discount rate

Less: Return on plan assets (actual)

Amortized unrecognized prior service cost

Plus: Actual > Expected return on plan assets

Amortized unrecognized gain or loss (corridor method used)

Pension Cost (PC)

Less: Employer contributions

Net pension cost (Net PC)

· If, the Net pension cost is (-) = Prepaid expense

· If, the Net pension cost is (+) = Accrued expense

Record Pension Cost

Pension expense	$$$	
Pension liability		$$$

Record Employer Contributions

Pension liability	$$$	
Cash		$$$

Unrecognized prior service cost = Change in PBO

$$\frac{\text{Unrecognized prior service cost}}{\text{Average years of service}} = \text{Amortized unrecognized prior service cost}$$

Example:

$$\text{Average years of service } 5 = \frac{\text{Years of service } \mathbf{20}}{\text{Total employees } 4}$$

Years of Service Calculation

Employees x Years of service remaining	1	x 3 yrs = 3	
+ Employees x Years of service remaining	2	x 5 yrs = 10	
+ Employees x Years of service remaining	1	x 7 yrs = <u>7</u>	
Years of service			**20**

Income Statement Activity

Unrecognized Gain (-) or Loss (+)
Beginning unrecognized gain (-) or Loss (+)
Amortized unrecognized gain (-) or Loss (+)
Projected benefit obligation gain (-) or Loss (+)
Plan assets gain (-) or Loss (+)
Ending unrecognized gain (-) or Loss (+)

Corridor Method

Unrecognized gain (-) or Loss (+)
Less: Greater of: (Projected benefit or Fair market value Plan assets) times 10%
Net unrecognized gain (-) or Loss (+)

$$\frac{\text{Net unrecognized gain (-) or loss (+)}}{\text{Average service life of employees}} = \text{Amortized unrecognized gain (+) or loss (-)}$$

- Amortized unrecognized gain (+) or loss (-) is a component of pension cost calculation.

Postemployment Benefits apply to:
- Former employees
- Inactive employees
- Their beneficiaries
- Covered dependents

Postemployment benefits include:
- Salary commitments
- Supplemental unemployment benefits
- **Severance** (FASB 112,43)
    - Installment payments apply if
        - Obligation occurs when employee services already rendered
        - Rights to benefits accumulate or vest
        - Payment of benefits is probable
        - Amount of benefits can be estimated
    - Expense the installment payments if no future commitment and/or obligation to perform a service.
        - Record expense and liability in the period of termination.
    - Disability related (workers compensation)
    - Job training and counseling
    - Continuation of health and life insurance

Terminology

1. Unrecognized prior service cost—the change in PBO.
2. Prior service cost—the current pension plan is amended to include prior service or a new plan is adopted and takes into account prior years of service
    a. PBO—projected benefit obligation is based on historical and future years of service.
3. Service cost—pension cost based on employee years of service.
4. Interest cost—interest earned on the pension plan payable to the employees at settlement date.
    a. Interest cost = PBO times Discount rate or Settlement rate
5. Settlement date is payment date.
6. Expected return on plan assets is the estimated rate of return on plan assets.
    a. Expected return on plan assets = Beginning plan assets at fair market value times Expected rate of return
7. ABO—accumulated benefit obligation is based on historical years of service.
    a. Future years of service and compensation are not included in the calculation.
8. Defined benefit plan—employer defines the benefits offered in the plan.
    a. Defined contribution plan—employer defines who contributes to the plan and how much.
9. PC—pension cost—actual cost payable to employees for the period.
10. MPL—minimum pension liability—unfunded pension cost (PC).
    a. Also referred to as the pension liability (PL).
    b. Minimum amount of pension cost due for the period.
11. EPL—excess pension liability—excess pension cost.
    a. The additional pension cost due after all activity has been record for the period.

Financial and Footnote Disclosure

1. Description of benefit plan
2. Components of pension cost
3. Rates

    a. Discount rate

    b. Compensation rate

    c. Expected rate of return on plan assets

4. The effect of a 1% increase on the assumed health care trend rate on:

    a. Service cost

    b. Interest expense or income

    c. Post benefit obligation

5. Reconciliation of beginning and ending balances

    a. PBO

    b. Plan assets

    c. Reconciliation of balance sheet versus income statement activity is *not* required.

6. Plan

    a. Gains or losses

    b. Income vs. expense

    c. Amendments

    d. Settlements

7. Effect of early retirement on benefits liabilities and savings

    a. Benefit payment

        i. Lump sum

        ii. Annuity (installment payments).

8. Savings on early termination of employee benefits

PROPERTY

Fixed Assets (FA)
- Capital expenditure for tangible property:
    - Real property
        - Land
        - Building
        - Leasehold Improvements
    - Personal property
        - Computer hardware
        - Computer software
        - Furniture and fixtures
        - Machinery
        - Natural resources—oil, gas, timber, minerals, precious gems, etc.
        - Office equipment
        - Capital assets—rentals, leases
        - Vehicles
- Asset basis
    - All cost associated with putting the asset in place for use
    - Capital improvements are capitalized, if the improvement improves the asset:
        - Quality
        - Efficiency (reduces cost)
        - Productivity

Real Property

Calculating cost:	Land	Buildings
Purchase price	$	$
Professional fees— legal and accounting	$	$
Architect, permits, etc.		$
Commissions		$
Interest expense—financing		$
Demolition, razing	$	
Excavation	$	
- Salvation proceeds	- $	
Landscaping		$
	Asset basis	Asset basis

- Land is not amortized.
- **Land Improvements**
    - Paving, fences, etc.—capitalized.
    - Upkeep and maintenance—expensed.
    - **Building**
        - Repairs and maintenance—expensed.
        - Replacements, modifications, and/or additions—capitalized.
            - If the cost can be determined, remove the old cost from the books.

- If the old cost cannot be determined, more information is required to determine how the old and new cost should be handled.
- Record the new replacement cost on books.
    - Examples of improvements
        - Roof
        - Fence
        - Sidewalk
        - Paving lot
        - Building infrastructure
- **Leasehold improvements**
    - Capitalize—leasehold improvement.
    - Amortized over the lesser of asset life or lease term
    - Examples of Leasehold Improvements
        - Additions
        - Improvements
        - Replacements
- Leasehold improvements are capitalized unless the landlord reimburses the tenant for cost of improvement in full or partial per tenant allowance agreement.
    - Reported as either:
        - Prepaid expense.
            - Amortized as a reduction of lease payments

Capitalization of Interest

- FASB 34—Capitalization of Interest
- Interest expense—construction financing
    - Construct for sale—expense interest cost
    - Construct for personal use
        - Capitalize interest cost to completion.
        - After completion—expense.
    - Calculate interest expense using the lesser of actual cost per amortization schedule or weighted average

Personal Property

Purchase cost
Freight In
Installation charges
Sales and use excise tax
Interest expense—construction financing
Total asset basis

Examples of personal property
- Computer hardware
- Computer software
- Furniture and fixtures
- Machinery
- Natural resources—oil, gas, timber, minerals, precious gems, etc.
- Office equipment
- Capitalize operating assets—rentals, leases
- Vehicles

Depletion Expense—Mining

Land cost
Development cost
Restoration cost
- Residual value
Depletion basis

Depletion basis   = Depletion rate times output = Depletion expense
Estimated removable units

- **Condemnation Awards**—Gain/loss is recognized.

       Gain/loss recognized by GAAP

       No gain/loss recognized for tax

     Award
     - Net book value
     Gain/loss recognized

- **Involuntary Conversion** -

       Gain/loss recognized by GAAP

       No gain/loss recognized for tax

     Proceeds
     - Net book value
     Gain/loss recognized

- **Property Dividends** are recorded at fair market value when declared.

     Example:
     Marketable security

Declared	Payment
Retained Earnings $35,000	Property Dividend Distributable $35,000
Property Dividend Distributable 35,000	Marketable Security 35,000
Marketable Security $5,000	
Gain—Disposal 5,000	

- **Donated assets** are recorded at fair market value when given and received.

Donor	Recipient
Donated asset $35,000	Asset $35,000
Asset 30,000	Additional paid in capital 35,000
Gain—Disposal 5,000	

RESEARCH AND DEVELOPMENT

Research and Development (R&D)
- Expensed.
- **Preproduction cost**
  - Research
  - Design, develop, test, and modify models, prototypes, etc.
  - Equipment
    - Expense if the sole purpose is R & D use
    - Capitalize if it has an alternate use, reevaluate its use and purpose.
- Excludes
  - Postproduction cost
  - Quality control (QC)
  - Trouble shooting
  - Routine improvements

SALES RECOGNITION—COMPLETED CONTRACTS

Completed Contracts—Method of Calculation

Step 1
Calculate percent complete based on accumulative cost to date divided by total cost of project.

$$\frac{\text{Cost to date (CTD)}}{\text{Total cost}} = \text{Percent (\%) complete}$$

Step 2
Calculate the current period cost.

$$
\begin{array}{l}
\text{Cost to date} \\
-\ \underline{\text{Previously recognized cost}} \\
\text{Current period cost}
\end{array}
$$

The current period cost is entered through the accounts payable system as the vendors submit their invoices for payment. A contract ledger system is maintained to track the cost.

Step 3
Calculate the progress billings.

$$
\begin{array}{l}
\phantom{\text{x}}\text{Percent \% complete} \\
\text{x}\ \underline{\text{Contract price}} \\
\phantom{\text{x}}\text{Progress billings}
\end{array}
$$

The gross profit is estimated when the project is priced. The total cost is the estimated total cost of the project. Gross profit is deferred revenue that will later be recognized as income when the project is complete.

Step 4
When the contract is complete, income is recognized.
Progress billings and construction in progress are closed to construction expense and revenue.

Example:
ABC Company agrees to a 3-year contract with a sales price of $1,200,000 and estimated cost to complete of $1,150,000.

Step 1
Calculate percent complete.

	Year 1	Year 2	Year 3
Cost to date (CTD)	$ 345	$ 920	$1,200
Total cost	1,150	1,150	1,200
% Complete	30%	80%	100%

Step 2

Calculate the current period cost.

	Year 1	Year 2	Year 3
Cost to date	$ 345	$ 920	$1,200
- *Previously recognized cost*	0	- 345	- 920
Current period cost	$ 345	$575	$ 280

Record current period cost using the accounts payable system.

	Year 1	Year 2	Year 3	Total
Construction in progress	**$345**	**$575**	**$280**	$1,200.00
Accounts payable	345	575	280	

Step 3

Calculate the progress billings. The progress billings are accumulative to date based on the contract price. And the current period progress billing is determined using previously recognized progress billing.

	Year 1	Year 2	Year 3
Contract price	$1,200	$1,200	$1,225
- *% Complete*	30%	80%	100%
Progress billing	$ 360	$960	$1,225
Less *previously recognized billings*	- 0	- 360	- 960
Current period billings	$ 360	$ 600	$ 265

	Year 1	Year 2	Year 3	Total
accounts receivable long-term contracts	**$360**	**$600**	**$265**	$1,225.00
Billings— long-term contracts	360	600	265	

Step 4

When the contract is complete, income is recognized.

	Year 1	Year 2	Year 3	Total
Billings— long-term contracts				$1,225
Construction revenue				1,225
Construction expense				$1,200
Construction in progress				1,200

Step 5

Record cash receipts. Record cash received during the contract term.

	Year 1	Year 2	Year 3	Year 4	Total
Cash	$300	$325	$375	$225	$1,225
Accounts receivable Long-term contracts	300	325	375	225	

SALES RECOGNITION—INSTALLMENT SALE

Installment Sale—Method of Calculation

Step 1
Calculate the gross profit amount of the contract.

> Contract price
> - Cost of sale
> Gross profit (GP)

Step 2
Calculate the gross profit percentage (GP %).

> $\dfrac{\text{Gross profit}}{\text{Contract price}}$ = Gross profit %

Step 3
Determine the cash collected (cash receipts) for the period.

Step 4
Calculate income recognized.

> Cash collected
> x Gross profit %
> Income recognized

Record income recognized.

Unearned revenue	$$$
Revenue	$$$

Income is recognized as cash is collected over the course of the agreement.

Step 5
Record installment sale. No income is recognized when the installment sale is recorded.

Installment sale receivable	$$$ (Installment sales price)
Inventory	$$$ (Cost of inventory)
Unearned revenue	$$$ (Deferred revenue)

Installment sale receivable. Installment sale accounts receivable may also be used.

Step 6
Determine deferred revenue. Deferred revenue is a percentage of accounts receivable. The beginning balance of installment sale receivable is equivalent to the installment sale. As such, the gross profit is a

percentage of the installment receivable or gross profit on sale. Income recognized as cash is collected reduces the deferred revenue balance.

Other terms used to refer to deferred revenue are:
1. Deferred gross profit
2. Deferred income

Accounts receivable—Installment sale

times Gross profit %

Deferred revenue—beginning

minus Income recognized

Deferred revenue - ending

AR—Installment sale—beginning balance	times GP % = deferred revenue
Installment sales	
- Payments (cash collected)	
- Write-off	
AR—installment—ending balance	times GP % = deferred revenue

Example

ABC Company agrees to a 3 year contract with a sales price of $1,200,000 and estimated cost to complete of $960,000.

Step 1
Calculate gross profit.

	Year 1	Year 2	Year 3
Contract Price	$1,200	$ 1,200	$1,225
- Total Cost	- 960	- 960	- 980
Gross Profit	$ 240	$ 240	$ 245

Step 2
Calculate gross profit percentage.

	Year 1	Year 2	Year 3
Gross profit	$ 240	$ 240	$ 245
Contract price	$1,200	$ 1,200	$1,225
Gross profit %'age:	20%	20%	20%

Step 3
Determine the cash collected (cash receipts) for the period.
Based on the recorded cash receipts.

	Year	Year 2	Year 3	Year 4	Total
Cash receipts	$300	$325	$375	$225	$1,225

Step 4
Calculate income recognized.

	Year 1	Year 2	Year 3	Year 4	Total
Cash receipts	$300	$325	$375	$225	$1,225
x *Gross profit %'age*	20%	20%	20%	20%	
Income recognized	**$ 60**	**$ 65**	**$ 75**	**$ 45**	**$ 245**
Unearned revenue	$ 60	$ 65	$ 75	$ 45	
Installment revenue	**60**	**65**	**75**	**45**	

Step 5
Record installment sale. The initial sale would be recorded as follows at the onset of the transaction.

Installment sale receivable	$1,200
Inventory	960
Unearned revenue	240

When the final sale and cost has been determined, an adjustment is recorded.

Installment sale receivable	$25
Inventory	20
Unearned revenue	5

Step 6
Determine deferred revenue.

Accounts receivable	
Installment sale	$1,200
x Gross profit %	x 20%
Deferred revenue—beg.	$ 240
Installment sale adjust	0
- *Income recognized*	- 60
Year 1 *Deferred revenue—ending $ 180*	
Installment sale adjust	0
- *Income recognized*	- 65
Year 2 *Deferred revenue - ending $ 115*	
Installment sale adjust	0
- *Income recognized*	- 75
Year 3 *Deferred revenue – ending $ 40*	
Installment sale adjust	5
- *Income recognized*	- 45
Year 4 *Deferred revenue - ending $ 0*	

Accounts receivable balance	
Installment sale received	$1,200
- *Cash receipt*	- 300
Year 1 *Installment sale received—ending $ 900*	
Installment sale received	0
- *Cash receipt*	- 325
Year 2 *Installment sale received—ending $ 575*	
Installment sale received	0
- *Cash receipt*	- 375
Year 3 *Installment sale received—ending $ 200*	
Installment sale received	25
- *Cash receipt*	- 225
Year 4 *Installment sale received—ending*	$ 0

Summary
1. Installment sale is used when collectability is uncertain.
2. Installment sale cannot be used under the following circumstances:
   a. If the sale results in a loss.
      i. Unless it was the sale of a business or investment property.
   b. Sale of inventory.
   c. Sale of stocks or securities trading on the stock exchange.

SALES RECOGNITION—PERCENTAGE OF COMPLETION

Percentage of completion—Method of Calculation

Step 1
Calculate percent complete based on accumulative cost to date divided by total cost of project.

$$\frac{\text{Cost to date (CTD)}}{\text{Total cost}} = \text{Percent (\%) complete}$$

Step 2
Calculate period cost.

$$
\begin{array}{l}
\ \text{Cost to date} \\
-\ \underline{\text{Previously recognized cost}} \\
\ \text{Current period cost}
\end{array}
$$

The period cost is entered through the accounts payable system as the vendors submit their invoices for payment. A contract ledger system is maintained to track the cost, progress billings and revenue.

Construction in progress	$$$$
Accounts payable	$$$$

Construction in progress is a work-in-progress account for long-term contracts. When the project is complete, the construction in progress account is reclassified to fixed assets (e.g., building) or inventory (e.g., airplane, ship, satellite, etc.) or for sale.

Step 3
Calculate the gross profit amount of the contract.

$$
\begin{array}{l}
\ \text{Contract price} \\
-\ \underline{\text{Total cost of project}} \\
\ \text{Gross profit (deferred revenue)}
\end{array}
$$

The estimated cost and revenue of the project is determined when the project is priced to the customer.

Step 4
Calculate the progress billings.

$$
\begin{array}{l}
\ \text{Contract price} \\
\times\ \underline{\% \text{ complete`}} \\
\ \text{Progress billings} \\
\text{Less } \underline{\text{previously recognized progress billings}} \\
\ \text{Current period billings}
\end{array}
$$

Progress billings are a function of the percent complete times the contract sales price. The progress billings are calculated on an accumulative-to-date basis. As such, the current period billings have to be determined.

Accounts receivable—long-term contracts	$$$	
Billings—long-term contracts		$$$

Step 5
Calculate income recognized over the term of the contract.

Gross profit
x <u>% Complete</u>
Accumulative income recognized
Less <u>previously recognized income</u>
Current period income recognized

Income recognized is a function of gross profit. Gross profit is deferred revenue that will later be recognized as income over the course of the project as it progresses toward completion. Gross profit is an accumulative amount, so the period income recognized has to be extrapolated based on income previously recognized.

Construction expenses	$$$	
Construction in progress	$$$	
Construction revenue		$$$

Step 6
Close the project when complete.

Billings—long-term contracts	$$$	
Construction in progress		$$$

Progress billings are closed to construction in progress when the project is complete.

Step 7
Record cash receipts when received over the term of the contract.

Cash	$$$	
Accounts receivable Long-term contracts		$$$

Example:

ABC Company agrees to a 3-year contract with a sales price of $1,200,000 and estimated cost to complete of $1,150,000.

Step 1

Calculate percent complete.

	Year 1	Year 2	Year 3
Cost to date (CTD)	$ 345	$ 920	$1,200
Total cost	1,150	1,150	1,200
% Complete	30%	80%	100%

Step 2

Calculate gross profit.

	Year 1	Year 2	Year 3
Contract price	$1,200	$ 1,200	$1,225
- Total cost	-,1,150	- 1,150	- 1,200
Gross profit	$ 50	$ 50	$ 25

Step 3

Calculate period cost.

	Year 1	Year 2	Year 3
Cost to Date	$ 345	$ 920	$1,200
- Previously recognized cost	0	- 345	- 920
Period cost	$ 345	$ 575	$ 280

Record period cost using the Accounts payable (AP) system.

	Year 1	Year 2	Year 3	Total
Construction in progress	$345	$575	$280	$1,200.00
Accounts payable	345	575	280	

Step 4

Calculate the progress billings.

	Year 1	Year 2	Year 3
Contract price	$1,200	$1,200	$1,225
- % Complete	30%	80%	100%
Progress billing	$ 360	$960	$1,225
Less previously recognized billings	- 0	- 360	- 960
Current period billings	$ 360	$ 600	$ 265

	Year 1	Year 2	Year 3	Total
Accounts receivable Long-term contracts	$360	$600	$265	$1,225.00
Billings—long-term contracts	360	600	265	

Step 5
Calculate income recognized.

	Year 1	**Year 2**	**Year 3**	**Total**
Gross Profit	$ 50	$ 50	$ 25	
x % Complete	30%	80%	100%	
Accumulative income recognized	$ 15	$ 40	$ 25	
Less previously recognized income	- 0	- 15	- 40	
Current period income recognized	$ 15	$ 25	$ - 15	

	Year 1	Year 2	Year 3	Total
Construction expense	$345	$575	$280	$1,200
Construction in progress	15	25	15	5
Construction revenue	360	600	265	$1,225

Step 6
Close accounts when the contract is complete.

	Year 1	**Year 2**	**Year 3**	**Total**
Billings—long-term contracts			$1,225	
Construction in progress			1,225	

Step 7

Record cash receipts.

	Year 1	**Year 2**	**Year 3**	**Year 4**	**Total**
Cash	$300	$325	$375	$225	$1,225
Accounts receivable Long-term contracts	300	325	375	225	

Summary overview

Balance Sheet
1. Records construction cost, progress billings, and cash received.

CIP	$$
Accounts payable	$$

| Accounts receivable Long-term contracts | $$ | |
| Billings Long-term contracts | | $$ |

| Cash | $$ | |
| Accounts receivable Long-term contracts | | $$ |

Income statement
2. Records income, expense, and closes the project.

Construction expense	$$	
CIP	$$	
Construction revenue		$$

| Billings on LT contracts | $$ | |
| Construction in progress | | $$ |

Progress billings are a contra-asset account and are used interchangeably with the following terms:
1. Progress billings
2. Billings on long-term contracts
3. Billings on construction contracts

Terms used interchangeably for revenue are:
1. Construction revenue
2. Revenue on long-term contracts

If Construction in progress > Progress billings

If construction in progress is greater than progress billings, there are unbilled expenses. The net effect is a debit represented as an asset (unbilled receivable) in the balance sheet.

If Construction in progress = Progress billings

If construction in progress is equal to progress billings, billings are properly reported. The net effect is zero (0) on the balance sheet and correctly reflects the amount due.

If Construction in progress < Progress billings

If construction in progress is less than progress billings, billings are overbilled. The net effect is a credit (billings—long-term contracts) represented as a liability in the balance sheet.

SEGMENT REPORTING

Segment Reporting (SFAS 131, ASC 280)
- The reporting of a business segment that has its own discrete financial activities.
- Applies to public, for-profit organizations
  - The standard applies to business entities trading on a domestic or foreign stock exchange, over-the-counter market including local and regional markets.
  - These businesses are required to file financial statements with the Securities and Exchange Commission for the purpose of issuing securities in a public market.
  - The standard does not apply to not-for-profit or nonpublic entities.
- Uses the management approach
  - Financial information of the segment is reviewed regularly by chief operating decision maker of the entity.
- **Segment reporting**
  - **Criteria**
    - If any of the following criteria are met, the entity is required to disclose certain financial information.
      - **10% Test**
        - If any one of the following is met, disclosure is required.
          - Assets
          - Net income ⎫ is ≥ 10% of the consolidated total revenue
          - Revenue ⎭
      - **75% Test**
        - If the following is met, disclosure is required.
          - The segment's third-party sales are ≥ 75% of consolidated third-party revenue.
    - The segment is required to disclose:
      - A full set of financial statements
      - Provide in the notes to the financial statements:
        - Product and services
        - Geographic locations
        - Major customers ≥ 10% of the consolidated total revenue

Example:

Segment	75% Test Unaffiliated Third-Party Revenue	Related Party Revenue	---------------- 10% Test ---------------- Total Revenue	Net Income	Assets
A	$3,000	$1,200	$4,200	$1,200	$15,900
B	200	300	500	– 300	6,700
C	650	150	800	250	4,420
D	800	600	1,400	510	$7,800
E	$1,200	1100	$2,300	- 900	6,500
F	$4,000	1000	$5,000	$2,600	$28,600
Total:	$9,850	Not applicable	$14,200	$3,360	$69,920

217

10% Test

Revenue: $14,200 x 10% = $1,420. Segments with revenue ≥ $1,420 are reported separately.
Net income: $ 3,360 x 10% = $336. Segments with net income ≥ $336 are reported separately.
Assets: $69,920 x 10% = $6,992. Segments with assets ≥ $6,992 are reported separately.

75% Test

Unaffiliated third-party revenue: $9,850 x 75% = $7,387.50
Segments with unaffiliated third-party revenue ≥ $7,387.50 are reported separately.

Therefore, segments A, D, E, and F financial information is to be reported separately in the financial statement and notes to the financial statements of the consolidated entity.

STOCK PLANS

Stock Plan

Grants the investor or employee the option to purchase the company's stock at a price below market. If the stock market price increases over the employee's service period, the employee receives an unrealized gain when the plan is exercised.

- **Grant date**
    - The date the stock plan is offered
    - The entry to record or recognize the offer depends upon the type of plan offered
- **Vested date**
    - The date when the employee is eligible to exercise the option to purchase
- **Exercise date**
    - The date the employee exercises his/her right to purchase the shares
- **Expiration date**
    - The date the offer expires
    - The offer to purchase the unexercised shares has ended
    - Employee is no longer eligible to purchase the unexercised shares
- **Service period**
    - The period in which the employee earns the right to exercise the option to purchase
- **Financial disclosure**
    - Number of shares offered under the plan
    - Number of shares exercised, forfeited, or expired
    - Weighted average—option price
    - Weighted average—fair market price
    - Average remaining life—stock plan
- **Type of stock plans**
    - **Compensatory stock plan**
        - Included as part of the employee compensation (form of payment).
            - Example:
                - Stock award plan is a share (equity) based plan.
                - Stock appreciation rights (SAR)
                    - Payable in shares of stock (equity) or cash (liability).
                        - If payable in cash, liability is recorded.
                        - Compensation expense is recorded as the change in market price until payment is made.
                    - SAR payment for past service can be exercised immediately.
                        - There is no required service period to be satisfied.
                        - Does not have to be allocated over a service period.
                    - Is an equity distribution
                        - Intrinsic method
                            - Uses the grant price.
                            - Amortize over service period.
                        - Fair value (FV) method
                            - Fair value of the stock is used
                            - Amortize over service period
        - Offered to key managers and officers of the corporation.

- Employer offers the employee stock options as an incentive for past or future performance or services.
- Manager and/or officer can purchase the stock < market value.
- Compensation expense is recognized.
  - Grant date—date the plan is offered
    - Record deferred compensation—contra-equity account

Deferred Compensation	$$	
Additional paid in capital—stock option		$$

  - Amortized (deferred compensation) over the service period until:
    - Expiration
    - Or the option is exercised prior to expiration.

Compensation expired	$$	
Deferred compensation		$$

  - Option—exercised—accepted, paid and stock issued.

Cash	$$	
Additional paid in capital—stock option	$$	
Common stock		$$
Additional paid in capital—common stock		$$

- **Noncompensatory Stock Plan**
  - Employee plans
    - Stock option plan
      - Employee must remain an employee for a certain period of time before he or she is eligible to purchase the company stock.
    - Stock subscription
    - Employee stock ownership plan
  - Stockholder plans
    - Stock rights
    - Stock option
  - Offered to employees as a benefit for years of service.
  - Not based on employee performance.
  - No compensation expense is recognized.
  - The stock issue is recorded as a normal stock issue.

Cash	$$	
Common stock.		$$
Additional paid in capital		$$

- **Dilutive Test**
  - Unexercised stock options
  - Applies when calculating earnings per share.

Example: Option to purchase 25,000 shares at $20 when the market price was $25.

$20 < $25

- **Test** (intrinsic value)**:** Option price < Market price
- **Determine the option purchase price** dollar amount.

$20 x 25,000 = $**500,000**

Option price x # of unexercised stock options = **Option purchase price**

- **Determine shares assumed acquired**

20,000

Option purchase price $500,000 = Shares assumed acquired
Market price per share $25

- **Determine dilutive shares**

Option shares 25,000
– Shares acquired - 20,000
Dilutive shares 5,000

- **Stock option**
  - An example of a derivative instrument
  - Seller gives the buyer the right to purchase a security
- **Investor** (purchaser)
  - Granted the option to purchase or sell shares at a specific price (strike price) within a certain period of time.
  - The option can be exercised anytime between purchase date and date of expiration.
    - Strike price—the exercise price in which a stock option can be brought or sold.
    - Put option—buyer agrees to purchase a security at an agreed upon price on or before a specific date with a certain expectation (for example, expects the price to decrease). If the expectation is met, the buyer has the right to sell the security at the agreed upon amount by a certain date.
    - Call option—buyer agrees to purchase the stock at a specific price on or before a specific date.
- **Employee stock ownership plan**
  - A form of retirement plan for the employee in which the company provides shares of stock to the employee as part of their compensation for services rendered.
  - No cost to the employee.
  - An account (trust) is set up for each employee who is participating in the plan.
  - The shares vest over time and become available to the employee after he or she leaves the company and the vested period has been earned.
  - The compensation expense is recorded at grant date.
- **Share based payments to nonemployees**
  - Is compensation in the form of a stock issue.
  - Classified as a liability.
  - For goods or services rendered by a third party.
  - Record the liability when payment is made.
  - Increase stockholder's equity.
  - And record an expense at FMV.

Example:

3/20 50 hours legal services are performed and completed by ABC Partnership. Payment is made by issuing 50 shares of common stock. Payment is due in 30 days.

4/19 payment: issued 50 Shares C.S. - $20 par at FMV of $25

$25	Legal services expense	1,250	
20	Common stock		1,000
$5	Additional paid in capital / common stock		250

Employee Stock Purchase Plan
- Option to purchase shares
- Deferred compensation
- A contra-equity account
- Recognized at grant date
- Amortized over the service period (vested period) using the straight line method unless exercised prior to expiration of service period.

Example:

10,000 shares common stock—Service period—3 years

- Par value $10   •   Option price $20   •   Market price $35 •   Fair value option price $27

Grant date

270,000	$27	10,000

Deferred compensation = Fair value stock option x   Number of option shares granted

Deferred compensation	270,000
Paid in capital—stock option	270,000

Amortize over the service period until expiration or until exercised prior to expiration.

270,000	90,000

Deferred compensation = Compensation expiration
Service paid 3 years

Compensation expiration	90
Deferred compensation	90

When the options are exercised, shares are issued, and payment is received.

10,000 Shares x Option price $20

$20 Cash	200,000		= $20 x 10,000 shares
$27	PIC stock option	$270,000	
$10	Common stock	$100,000	
	Additional paid in capital—Common stock	$370,000	Stockholder's equity increased $200,000

STOCK TRANSACTIONS

Assets
Less: Liabilities
 Stockholder's equity

Stockholders' Equity

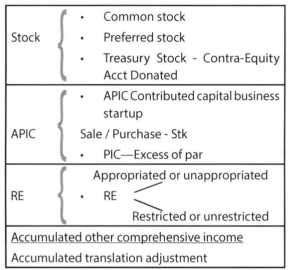

Stock	• Common stock • Preferred stock • Treasury Stock - Contra-Equity Acct Donated
APIC	• APIC Contributed capital business startup Sale / Purchase - Stk • PIC—Excess of par
RE	• RE — Appropriated or unappropriated / Restricted or unrestricted
Accumulated other comprehensive income	
Accumulated translation adjustment	

Hierarchy of Corporate Structure

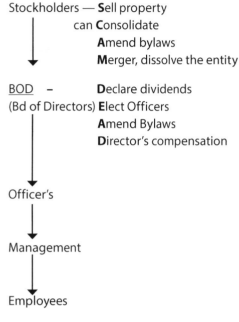

Stockholders — **S**ell property
    can **C**onsolidate
      Amend bylaws
      Merger, dissolve the entity

BOD – **D**eclare dividends
(Bd of Directors) **E**lect Officers
      Amend Bylaws
      Director's compensation

Officer's

Management

Employees

- Stock certificate
  - Name
  - Address
  - Number of shares
  - Rights of shareholder
    - Stock rights—voting
    - Distribution of earnings (dividends)
    - Purchase additional shares—preemptive right
    - Asset upon liquidation
    - Proxy form
    - Rights to financial reports
    - Shareholders' ledger—list all shareholders

- **Securities Disclosure Requirements**
  - Dividends
  - Liquidation preferences
  - Participation rights
  - Call prices and dates
  - Conversion options
  - Exercise prices and dates
  - Sinking fund requirements
  - Voting rights
  - Terms for issuing additional shares

- Double taxation
  - Corporation is taxed on earnings distributed.
  - Shareholder is taxed on the receipt of earnings received or not.

Retained Earnings (RE)

Financial Statement (FS) Disclosure Notes to Financial Statements

	Financial Statement (FS)	Disclosure Notes to Financial Statements
• Unrestricted	X	
• Unappropriated	X	
• Restricted	X	X
• Appropriated	X	

- Restricted or appropriated retained earnings
- A reclassification of equity
  - No change in stockholders equity
- Legal restriction
- GAAP requirement
- Recorded as a contractual requirement (e.g., expected lawsuit)
- Or at the board of director's request (e.g., a Dividend restriction)

Recording restricted retained earnings.

Unrestricted retained earnings or retained earnings	$$	
Restricted retained earnings		$$

Appropriated RE

Unappropriated RE or retained earnings	$$	
Appropriated retained earnings		$$

- Once the appropriation requirement has been satisfied, the appropriation is reversed.

Appropriated retained earnings	$$	
Unappropriated retained earnings or retained earnings		$$

Terminology
- Authorized
  - Stock is legally available for sale (issue).
  - Authorized to sell (issue).
- Grant—offer to purchase.
- Exercise—buyer accepts offer.
  - Buyer submits payment.
  - Seller issues stock.
- Issue—stock is distributed to shareholder when paid (capital distribution).
- Stockholder or Shareholder
  - Owner of corporate shares of stock.
  - Has certain rights and ownership in the corporation.
- Outstanding shares—number of shares in shareholders possession.
- Stock value
  - Par—value assigned to a share of stock.
  - No par—no value is assigned to a share of stock.
  - Stated—the given par value of a share of stock. When no par value is given. A stated value is assigned.
- APIC (additional paid in capital) or PIC—excess of par (paid in capital in excess of par)

- Cash or noncash exchange or capital contribution.
  - PIC—amount received for issuing stock.
  - PIC—excess of par—amount received in excess of par value.
  - APIC—amount received for common or preferred stock issue exceeding par value.

Stock types:
- CS—common stock—general ownership interest in a corporation.
  - Voting
  - Nonvoting
- PS—preferred stock
  - Preferential treatment over common stock regarding dividends.
    - Preferred stock is paid first.
      - Characteristics
        - Cumulative
        - Noncumulative
        - Participating
        - Nonparticipating
        - Convertible
        - Callable
        - With detachable warrants
        - Without detachable warrants
- TS—treasury stock
  - Corporation buys back (reacquires) its stock.
    - Contra-equity account—decreases stockholder's equity.
      - The stock is either:
        - Held in treasury
        - Retired
    - Par or cost method is used to record the reacquired stock.

Common Stock (CS)

- General ownership interest in a corporation.
- **Stock issued at premium**

Cash	Proceeds
C.S.	Par or stated value
APIC	Proceeds in excess of par or stated value (PIC—excess of par may also be used instead of APIC).

- **Stock issued at Discount**

Cash	Proceeds
APIC	Proceeds less than par or stated value (PIC—excess of par may also be used instead of APIC).
CS	Par or Stated value

- **Stock Retirement**

  Under par value method

CS	Par or stated value.
TS	Par or stated value.

Under cost method

CS	Par or stated value.
APIC	Amount excess of par or stated value.
TS	stock value under cost method.

Stock Split
- Declared by board of directors
  - Affects the number of outstanding shares
  - Increases marketability of stock
  - No change in stockholders' equity
    - Stock split increases the number of share outstanding and decreases par or stated value.
    - Reverse split decreases the number of shares outstanding and increases par or stated value.
  - Change in shareholder's equity occurs when the change in shares is *not* in proportion to the change in stated or par value.
- Recorded in the notes to financial statements indicating the change in shares and par or stated value.

Example:

$$100,000 \quad : \quad \$5$$

$$\text{2:1 Stock split} = \frac{2}{1} \text{ x \# of o/s shares:} \frac{1}{2} \text{ x Par or stated value.}$$

100,000 Shares at \$5 par = 500,000
↓
200,000   at \$2.50 par = 500,000
Increase number of shares decrease par value of stock   } *No change in stockholder's equity.*

$$100,000 \quad : \quad \$5$$

$$\text{1:2 Reverse Split} = \frac{1}{2} \text{ x \# of o/s shares:} \frac{2}{1} \text{ x Par or stated value.}$$

100,000 Shares at \$5 par = 500,000
↓
50,000   at \$10 par = 500,000
Decrease number of shares increase par value of stock   } *No change in stockholder's equity*

$$100,000 \quad : \quad \$5$$

$$\text{5:1 Stock Split} = \frac{5}{1} \text{ x \# of o/s shares:} \frac{1}{5} \text{ x Par or stated value.}$$

100,000 Shares at \$5 par = 500,000
↓
500,000 Shares at \$1 par = 500,000   } *No change in stockholder's equity*

Preferred Stock (PS)—Overview
- Authorized
- Issued
- Participating
- Nonparticipating
- Cumulative
- Noncumulative
- Convertible
- Callable
- With detachable warrants
- Without detachable warrants

Preferred Stock
- Has certain preferences or rights not associated with common stock
- Has preference regarding dividend payments
  - Paid before common stock dividends
- Issued
  - Stocks are issued when sold and paid in full
  - Increases shareholder's equity

Cash	Proceed
PS	Par value
APIC	Difference

Preferred Stock
- Participating—participates with common stock regarding dividend distributions.
- Calculate preferred and common stock dividends distributed.

Example:
Paid $300 cash dividend that must be allocated between PS and CS.
PS is participating.

*CS 100 shares—$25 par times 8% = $200/$240 times **$60** = $50 = $250*

*PS 100 shares—$5 par times 8% = $40/$240 times **$60** = $10 = 50*

Total $ 240   **$60**

Paid cash dividend—300

Allocate the difference $ 60 to PS and CS

Declared		*Paid*	
Retained earnings 300		*PS dividend distribution*	*50*
PS dividend distribution	*50*	*CS dividend distribution*	*250*
CS dividend distribution	*250*	*CS*	*250*
		PS	*50*

- *Nonparticipating—PS does not participate with CS regarding distribution of earnings (dividends).*
- *Cumulative—unpaid dividends accumulate.*
  - *Declared and not paid—accrue (record liability) in financial statements.*
  - *Paid and not declared—record in notes to financial statements or parenthetical disclosure.*

Example:
No dividends were declared or paid during the first 2 years. Year 3 $20k was paid but not declared.

Year 1—*3,000 PS shares x $100 par x 5% = 15,000 Unpaid and not declared*
Year 2   *= 15,000 Unpaid and not declared*
Year 3—*Paid $20,000 Cash Dividend = 15,000 Unpaid and not declared*
                                     $ 45,000 Total dividends unpaid and not declared.
                                     – 20,000 paid but not declared
                                     $25,000 Dividend in arrears requires note disclosure.

Treasury Stock
- The reacquisition (buyback) of a company's shares
  - A contra-equity account
  - Corporation reacquires its own stock to:
    - Meet employee stock contracts
    - Meet merger requirements
    - Affect earnings per share by decreasing the number of outstanding shares
    - Prevent a takeover.
- (2) Methods are used to record treasury stock
  - Par method
    - Reacquire > Original issue = Loss (retained earnings)
    - Reacquire < Original issue = Gain (PIC–TS)
    - Later, reissue T.S.
    - Reissue > Original issue = Gain (PIC–T.S.)
    - Reissue < Original issue = Loss (retained earnings)
  - Cost method
    - Reacquire vs Original issue—Not applicable.
      - The reacquired stock is recorded at its purchase price.
    - Later, reissue treasury stock
    - Reissue > Reacquire cost = Gain (PIC–T.S.)
    - Reissue < Reacquire cost = Loss (retained earnings)

Under both the par and cost methods stockholder' equity decreases when the stock is purchased back. Likewise, stockholders' equity increases or decreases when the treasury stock is reissued for an amount greater or less than par value or cost.

Treasury Stock—Par Method
Example: <u>Original stock Issue</u>
                     Issued 1,000—CS shares with a $5 par value for $20 per share.

$20	Cash 20,000	= 1,000 x $20
5	C.S.	5,000 = 1,000 x $5
15	PIC—Excess par	15,000 = 1,000 x $15 ($20—$5)

The company

                                       $18   <   *$20 =* **$2**

Acquires (buys back) 200 shares at $18:   *Acquire*   <   *Original Issue = PIC—T.S.*

Buy back shares for an amount less than original issue price resulting in a gain ($2) credited to PIC—TS

$5 TS		$1,000= 200 x $5		
$15 PIC—Excess par	3,000			= 200 x $15
$18	Cash	3,600		= 200 x $18
$2	PIC–TS	400		= 200 x $2

Reissue (resell) 150 shares of the 200 acquired for $27:

$27 > $20 = $7
Resold > Original issue = PIC–TS

Resold the buyback shares for an amount greater than original issue price resulting in a gain ($7) credited to PIC—TS

$27	Cash	$4,050	= 150 x $27
$5 TS		750	= 150 x $5
$15 PIC—Excess par		2,250	= 150 x $15
$7 PIC–TS		1,050	= 150 x **$7**

Reissue the remaining 50 shares for $16:

$16 < $20 = **$4**
Resold < Original issue = retained earnings

Resold the buyback shares for an amount less than original issue price resulting in a loss ($2) debited to RE (retained earnings).

RE	$ 200		= 50 x **$4**
$16 Cash	800		= 50 x $16
$5	T.S.	250	= 50 x $5
$15	PIC—Excess Par	750	= 50 x $15

Treasury Stock—Cost Method

Example: *Original stock issue*

Issued 1,000—CS shares with a $5 par value for $20 per share.

$20 Cash	20,000	= 1,000 x $20
5	C.S.	5,000 = 1,000 x $5
15	PIC—Excess par 15,000 = 1,000 x $15 ($20—$5)

The company

Acquires (buys back) 200 Shares @ $18:
Buyback shares are recorded at purchase price. And, are not adjusted against the original issue price.

$18 TS	*$3,600*	*= 200 x $18*
$18	*Cash 3,600*	*= 200 x $18*

Reissue (resold) 150 shares of the 200 acquired for $27:

*$27 > $18 = **$9***
Resold > Acquired = PIC–TS

Resold the buyback shares for an amount greater than buyback cost resulting in a gain ($9) credited to PIC—TS

$27 Cash	*$4,050*	*= 150 x $27*
$18	*T.S. 2,700*	*= 150 x $18*
$ 9	*PIC—TS 1,350*	*= 150 x **$9***

Reissue the remaining 50 shares for $16:

*$16 > $18 = **$2***
Resold > Acquired = retained earnings

Resold the buyback shares for an amount less than buyback cost resulting in a loss ($2) debited to RE (retained earnings).

$ 2 retained earnings	*$ 100*	*= 50 x **$2***
$16 cash	*800*	*= 50 x $16*
$18	*TS 900*	*= 50 x $18*

Stock Rights

- Grant date
  - An offer is made to purchase shares of stock less than fair market value (FMV)
    - No journal entry is recorded
      - A memo is made regarding the offer to purchase additional shares
- Exercise date
  - Stock rights are exercised.
  - Payment is received.
  - Stock is issued.
  - Journal entry is made to record payment.

Cash received	
CS	Par Value
APIC–CS	Delta

Stock Subscription

- Subscription (offer) to purchase CS or PS stock less than fair market value on credit.

Example:

Subscribe   *300 Shares - $5 par at $25, 15% down payment   Market value $30*

Down payment *(15%)*   **Balance—paid in full** *(P I F) (85%)*

- *Record Subscription*   · *Stock is issued.*
- *Increase stockholders' equity*   · *Record stock issue and payment.*
- *No stock is issued.*

	Cash	$6,375
	Subscription receivable	6, 375

Cash		**$1,125** = *300 shares x $25 = $7500 x 15% =* **$1,125**		
Subscription receivable	6,375	CS subscribe	$1,500	
CS subscribe	1,500	APIC-stock sub	6,000	
APIC stock subscription	6,000	CS	1,500	
		APIC-CS	1,600	

Cancel subscription or record default in payment

CS Subscribe	$1,500
APIC stock subscription	6,000
Subscription	6,375
Subscription fee payable	500
Refundable subscription deposit	625

Convertible Stock

No change in stockholder's equity at conversion date.

Example:

Issued: 5 Shares PS—$90 Par at $100 = $500
- *Each share of PS converts into 3 shares of C S at $25 par*
- *Record the PS issue*

$100 Cash	$500	
90	PS	450
10	APIC PS	50

Date of Conversion

The PS is converted into CS

3 Shares CS x 5 shares PS = 15 x $25 = $375
Shares par

Unit Price

$90	P.S.	$450		
10	APIC PS	50		· *No effect on stockholder's equity*
25	CS	375		
Λ	APIC CS	125		

Callable Shares
- Corporation has the option to buy back its shares at a specific price.
- Call price > Issue price = Loss (retained earnings) • Paid more than issue price.
- Call price < = Gain (PIC) • Paid less than issue price.
- Stockholder's equity decreases at call date.

Example:

Issued: *5 shares of preferred stock, $100 par at $110*

Unit Price

$110	*Cash*	*$550*		*= 5 shares x $110*
100	***PS***	***500***	}	*Stockholders' equity increased $550*
10	***APIC PS***	***50***		

Called 5 shares at $105 *< Issue price $110 = Gain (PIC)*

Unit Price

$100	***PS***	***$500***			
10	***APIC PS***	*50*			
105		*Cash*	*525*	}	*Stockholders' equity decreased $525 = $500 + 50 - 25*
5		***PIC PS***	***25***		

Called at $115 *> Issue price $110 = Loss (RE)*

Unit Price

Retained equity	***$ 25***			
$100 ***PS***	***500***		}	*Stockholders' equity decreased $575*
10 ***APIC PS***	***50***			
115	*Cash*	*575*		

Donated Capital
- Third party contributes asset to the corporation.
- Increases APIC—donated capital account.

Examples of donated capital

	Receipt		**Later, Sold**		
Stock:	Investment Corporate stock	75	Cash	110	
	APIC-donated capital	75	Investment Corporate stock		75
			Gain—Disposal		35
Equipment:	Equipment	75	Cash	60	
	APIC—donated capital	75	Equipment net of accumulated depreciation	45	

			Gain—disposal		15

Property:	Land	50	Cash	175
	Building	200	Land	50
	APIC—donated capital	250	Building net of accumulated depreciation	100
			Gain—disposal	25

Quasi Reorganization
- Allows a company to eliminate retained earnings deficit.
- Authorized by stockholders.
  - Or creditor's if applicable.
- Revalue assets and liabilities to FMV.
  - Recognize unrealized gains and losses.
- Decrease par value of the company's stock.
- Eliminate retained earnings deficit.

Common stock	$$		at par value
Retained earnings	$$		eliminate deficit
APIC	$$		delta

Example:
Company had a retained earnings deficit of $100,000.
Common stock 20,000 shares issued, par value $20.

1. *Revalue assets and liabilities to fair market value.*

Property and plant $25,000
*   Unrealized gain $25,000*

Unrealized loss $10,000
*   Equipment $10,000*

2. *Reduce par value of common stock to $15.*

CS $100,000   = 20,000 shares x ($20 minus $15)
*   APIC   100,000*

3. *Eliminate retained earnings deficit.*

Credit Retained earnings $115,000 = $100,000 retained earnings deficit + (Net unrealized gain $15,000)

SOURCES OF INFORMATION

Fess-Warren. *Accounting Principles—Fourteenth Edition*. Tennessee: South-Western Publishing Co., 1984.

Kieso, Donald E., PhD, CPA, and Jerry J. Weygandt PhD, CPA. *Intermediate Accounting—Fifth Edition*. Marblehead, Massachusetts: John Wiley & Sons, Inc., 1986.

Spiceland, J. David, Jim Sepe, and Lawrence Tomassini. *Intermediate Accounting – Fourth Edition*. McGraw/Hill Irwin, 2007.

Weston, J. Fred, and Eugene F. Brigham. *Essentials of Managerial Finance—Eighth Edition*. Oak Brook, Illinois: The Dryden Press, 1987.

Whittington, O. Ray, PhD, CPA, PhD – 2016 *Wiley CPAexcel Exam Review Study Guide – Financial Accounting and Reporting*. Marblehead, Massachusetts: John Wiley & Sons, Inc., 2016.

ASC 205 – Presentation of Financial Statements
ASC 205-20 – Discontinued Operations
ASC 210 – Balance Sheet
ASC 215 – Statement of Shareholder Equity
ASC 220 – Comprehensive Income
ASC 225 – Income Statement
ASC 225-20 – Extraordinary and Unusual Items
ASC 230 – Statement of Cash Flows
ASC 235 – Notes to Financial Statements
ASC 250 – Accounting Changes and Error Corrections
ASC 255 – Changing Prices
ASC 260 – Earning per Share
ASC 280 – Segment Reporting
ASC 300 – Assets
ASC 320 – Investments – Debt and Equity Securities
ASC 320-10-05 – Overview of Investments in Other Entities
ASC 320-10-35 – Reclassification of Investments in Securities
ASC 320-10-35 – Transfer of Securities: Between Categories
ASC 323-10 – Equity Method Investments
ASC 325-20 – Cost Method Investments
ASC 330 – Inventory
ASC 350-20 – Goodwill
ASC 350-30 – Intangibles Other than Goodwill
ASC 350-40 – Internal-Use Software
ASC 350-50 – Website Development Cost
ASC 360 – Property, Plant, and Equipment
ASC 360-10-35 - Depreciation
ASC 405 – Liabilities
ASC 430 – Deferred Revenue
ASC 450 – Contingencies
ASC 450-20 – Loss Contingencies

ASC 450-30 – Gain Contingencies
ASC 470 – Debt
ASC 505 – Equity
ASC 505-10 – Overall
ASC 505-20 – Stock dividends and stock splits
ASC 505-30 – Treasury stock
ASC 505-50 – Equity based payments to non-employees
ASC 600 – Revenue
ASC 605 – Revenue Recognition
ASC 700 – Expenses
ASC 705 – Cost of Sales and Services
ASC 715-30 – Defined Benefits Plans - Pension
ASC 718 – Compensation-Stock Compensation
ASC 730 – Research and Development
ASC 740 – Income Taxes
ASC 805 – Business Combinations
ASC 810 – Consolidation
ASC 810 – Noncontrolling Interests
ASC 815 – Derivatives and Hedging
ASC 820 – Fair Value Measurements and Disclosures
ASC 825 – Financial Instruments
ASC 830 – Foreign Currency Matters
ASC 830-20 – Foreign Currency Transactions
ASC 830-30 – Translation of Financial Statements
ASC 835 – Interest
ASC 840 – Leases
ASC 840-20 – Operating Leases
ASC 840-30 – Capital Leases
ASC 840-40 – Sale-Leaseback Transactions
ASC 850 – Related Party Disclosures
ASC 855 – Subsequent Events
ASC 915 – Development stage entities
ASC 954 – Health care entities
ASC 958 – Not-for-profit entities

Printed in the United States
By Bookmasters